# THE
# Lighthouse
### HANDBOOK
# Hudson River &
# New York Harbor

# THE Lighthouse HANDBOOK

# Hudson River & New York Harbor

# THE Lighthouse HANDBOOK
# Hudson River & New York Harbor

{ THE ORIGINAL LIGHTHOUSE FIELD GUIDE }

By Jeremy D'Entremont

CIDER MILL PRESS

BOOK
PUBLISHERS

Kennebunkport, Maine

13-Digit ISBN: 978-1-60433-040-3
10-Digit ISBN: 1-60433-040-6

This book may be ordered by mail from the publisher. Please include $2.50 for postage and handling.
Please support your local bookseller first!

Books published by Cider Mill Press Book Publishers are available at special discounts for bulk purchases in the United States by corporations, institutions, and other organizations. For more information, please contact the publisher.

Cider Mill Press Book Publishers
"Where good books are ready for press"
12 Port Farm Road
Kennebunkport, Maine 04046

Visit us on the web!
www.cidermillpress.com

Design by PonderosaPineDesign.com, Vicky Vaughn Shea
Typography Baskerville MT, NumbersStyle Two, Post Antiqua, Salmiak, Swiss 721, Today SB

Printed in China

1 2 3 4 5 6 7 8 9 0
First Edition

This book is dedicated to all lighthouse keepers, past and present, including the modern-day lighthouse preservationists who have fought so valiantly to keep the lights burning, literally and figuratively.

## KEY TO ICONS

For each lighthouse in the book, icons are used to help convey information on accessibility, as follows:

 indicates the lighthouse can be reached by car.

 indicates the lighthouse may be viewed from a public cruise or charter.

+ means a boat ride to an island plus a car or other transportation are needed.

 indicates that a view (possibly distant) from shore is possible.

 means a significant walk is necessary to reach the lighthouse.

 means the site is closed to the public, even though it may be reachable by car.

 means that the lighthouse and/or keeper's house are open to the public, at least on a limited basis.

 means there are overnight accommodations.

# Acknowledgments

My sincere thanks to all who helped with this book, in particular Pat Ralston of the Save Esopus Lighthouse Commission, Doris Hubbard and family, Scott Schubert and family, Patrick Landewe of the Saugerties Lighthouse, and all the lighthouse keepers and family members who have shared their stories with me and other authors.

Thanks also to the staffs of several local libraries and historical societies, as well as the Hudson River Maritime Museum and the National Archives, who helped by providing valuable documents and clippings.

Thanks as always to the men and women of the U.S. Coast Guard, who have unfailingly provided information and assistance when asked.

Finally, thanks to the authors whose writings on these lighthouses have been a help and inspiration, including Jim Crowley, Robert G. Bachand, J. Candace Clifford and Mary Louise Clifford, and Rick Tuers, among others. Special recognition also goes to the late Hudson River historian Ruth Reynolds Glunt.

# Contents

# PART ONE
# New York's Illustrious Harbor

New York Harbor ranks as one of the most important bodies of water in North America in terms of its historical interest and its commercial importance. The term *New York Harbor* is generally applied to an area that includes Upper New York Bay, Lower New

York Bay, the East River, the Kill Van Kull, Newark Bay, the Arthur Kill, the Narrows, Jamaica Bay, Raritan Bay, and the Harlem River. With more than twelve hundred square miles of area and two hundred forty miles of shipping channels, it's no surprise that the busy harbor area has been home to so many lighthouses and lightships over the past 250 years.

The native Lenape Algonquian people fished in the area for centuries before the arrival of Europeans. The Dutch, who traded with the natives for valuable pelts, established the first permanent European settlement in the harbor in 1624, on Governors Island. The province of New Netherland expanded in the next few years to several other settlements, including the southern end of Manhattan in 1626. The fort built there and the surrounding village, known as New Amsterdam, was the seed of the largest metropolis in North America.

New Amsterdam came under British control in 1664. The Dutch later recaptured it, but a 1674 treaty left it firmly in the hands of the British. Renamed New York after the English duke of York and Albany, the city blossomed as a center for trade, largely because of its commodious waterways.

One of the nation's earliest lighthouses was established at the harbor's entrance at Sandy Hook in 1764, testifying to the port's significance. Maritime commerce and immigration continued to transform the city through the nineteenth century, especially after the opening of the Erie Canal in 1825. By the 1840s, more tonnage was coming through the port of New York than all the other significant harbors in the country combined.

Coney Island Light

The St. George waterfront of Staten Island was the historic home of a U. S. Lighthouse Service depot that supplied the nation's lighthouses for more than a century, beginning in 1862. This site, adjacent to the Staten Island Ferry terminal, was chosen in the 1990s to be the home of the National Lighthouse Museum. The museum project appears to be sadly on permanent hold, due to a lack of funding and other complications.

The following pages tell the stories of twenty-four lighthouses and lightships established in New York Harbor between 1764 and 1990. The lighthouses at Sandy Hook and the Navesink Highlands are among the nation's most historic and visitor-friendly. Some of the other lighthouses in this area are difficult to view up close, but I've provided suggestions when possible. Difficulty of access has never deterred the most ardent lighthouse hunters.

The enormous bivalve first-order lens on display at the Navesink station is worth a special trip, as are the extensive and informative exhibits at that location. It was the magnificent lens from Navesink that helped spark my own interest in lighthouses, back in the 1970s when I worked at the Boston Museum of Science and the lens was on display there. Its crystalline beauty and awe-inspiring workmanship planted a seed in my imagination that has grown ever since.

Even if you can't get to see them yourself, I hope you'll enjoy reading about these places, and I hope you'll also enjoy learning about the dedicated men and women who devoted themselves to keeping these lights. Most notable is Kate Walker of Robbins Reef, a tiny woman who was a tower of dependability and strength, as solid as any rock in the sea.

Walker rightfully holds a place among our most celebrated keepers, but the stories of many others are compelling in their own right. One of my personal favorites is Ed Burge, longtime keeper at West Bank and other locations. Burge scoffed at romantic notions of lightkeeping. "Peace and quiet? A lighthouse is about the noisiest place in the world!" he once told a reporter. Life was rugged, indeed, and often noisy in times of storms, particularly at West Bank and the harbor's other offshore stations.

There are a number of references to range lights in the text. Range lights are light pairs that indicate a specific position when they are in line. In other words, when mariners see the lights vertically in line, with the rear light above the front light, they are on the range line. In some sections of the book, there are references to range light structures that no longer exist. Not all of those lights are described in detail in separate sections, as little information is available beyond what is already included in the text.

I hope you'll get the opportunity to experience some of these fascinating places for yourself. If your time is limited, I strongly recommend visits to Sandy Hook Lighthouse and the Navesink Twin Lights, as well as a cruise on the Staten Island ferry or a sightseeing boat in New York Harbor. Anything after that is icing on the cake.

# New York Harbor Lights

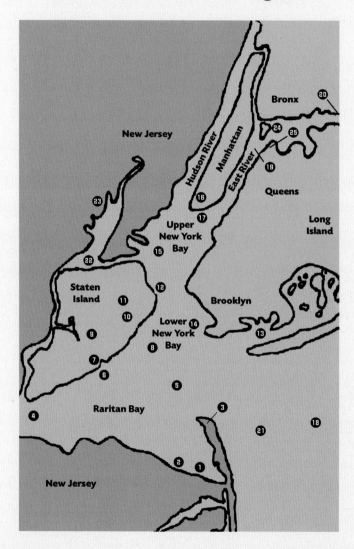

# NAVESINK TWIN LIGHTS

As early as the 1740s, the prominent hills known as the Navesink Highlands (the word *Navesink* comes from a Native American word for "fishing place") were used as a site for a warning beacon. Near the site of the present light station, a beacon was erected, with pots of whale oil to be lighted if the French fleet was approaching New York. The system was retired after it was lighted accidentally and nobody noticed.

At two hundred and sixty-six feet above sea level, Beacon Hill in the Highlands is the highest point on the nation's Atlantic coastline south of Mount Desert Island in Maine. Other signal beacons were later employed on the site; early references to a lighthouse at the Highlands prior to 1828 most likely refer to these structures. During the American Revolution, the Americans maintained a lookout post to monitor British troop movements in and out of New York Harbor.

Congress appropriated $30,000 in May 1826 for three new light stations in the New York City area: one on Staten Island, one in Princess Bay, and a twin light station on the Highlands of Navesink. Two and three-quarter acres of suitable land at the Highlands was purchased from Nimrod Woodward for $600.

Charles H. Smith of Stonington, Connecticut, constructed the original light station buildings at the Highlands in 1827–28 for $8,440, and the lighting apparatus was installed by David Melville of Newport, Rhode

**Fascinating Fact**

In 1841, the Navesink station became the first light station in the United States to use Fresnel lenses, a revolutionary type of lighthouse lens invented in France in 1822.

Island, for $1,850. The original station consisted of two octagonal bluestone towers, three hundred twenty feet apart, with a dwelling between them. The first keeper was Joseph Doty of Somerville, New Jersey.

The Navesink Light Station, about four miles south of the lighthouse established at Sandy Hook in 1764, became the primary landfall light for vessels heading to New York Harbor. The station was given two lights to make it easy for mariners to differentiate it from Sandy Hook Light and the Sandy Hook Lightship offshore.

An 1838 inspection report described the lighting apparatus, which consisted of six lamps and reflectors producing a fixed white light (the north tower) and a revolving apparatus of fifteen lamps and reflectors producing a flashing white light (the south tower). The report indicated that the towers had problems with leaks, but the dwelling was in good repair.

In 1838, Congress authorized Commodore Matthew C. Perry to travel to Europe to examine the lighthouses and lighting systems in use there. The Fresnel lens had been invented in Paris in 1822, and this efficient type of lens with multiple prisms that bent the light into a powerful beam was in widespread use in lighthouses by the time of Perry's trip.

Perry was instructed to purchase a fixed first-order lens and a revolving second-order lens from Henry Lepaute of Paris. The two lenses were installed at the Navesink station at a cost of $24,000 after the lanterns were extensively refitted in 1840–41. Both of the new lenses were in operation by March 1841. Stephen Pleasonton, in charge of the nation's lighthouses, wrote to the chairman of the House Committee on Commerce in December 1841:

*The cost of these lenses . . . is nothing compared to the beauty and excellence of the light they afford. They appear to be the perfection of apparatus for light-house purposes, having in view only the superiority of the light, which is reported by the pilots to be seen in clear weather a distance of forty miles. . . . There are some drawbacks, however, in relation to their management, which would render them unfit for use in the United States upon a large scale, there being but one lamp which supplies all the light, with three or four concentric wicks, and this lamp . . . is very apt to get out of order, and the light become extinguished, if the keeper be not an intelligent mechanic, and capable at all times of making the necessary repairs.*

*We have been fortunate as to obtain such a keeper at Navesink, a man who can make every part of the machinery, both of the lamp and the clock-work, and apply it in case of necessity without the least delay, and he is a man, moreover, who appears to take a pride in doing his duty in the best and most satisfactory manner. He has attached to him three assistants, taken from the class of seafaring men, who watch alternately every two hours through each night . . .*

In 1851, Lieutenant David D. Porter of the U.S. Navy proclaimed that the twin lights were the "only perfect lights on our coast, not only as regards regularity in lighting, but in the brilliancy of the light." The revolving light could be seen as far as thirty miles on a clear night. "These two are the best lights that I am acquainted with," wrote Porter, "and the mariner can steer for them with perfect confidence, knowing they will always be lighted in time, and even in thick weather will warn him of danger."

Also in 1851, the investigating committee of the Lighthouse Board

Early 1900s view of Navesink Twin Lights Station

received a letter from Jonathan Howland, the captain of the vessel that brought oil and other supplies to East Coast lighthouses. He reported that the lighting apparatus was in poor condition, and the keepers were poorly trained. The principal keeper, James D. Hubbard, had only one night of instruction from his predecessor.

Howland felt that three properly trained keepers would be sufficient, rather than the five then employed. The Lighthouse Board decided that a

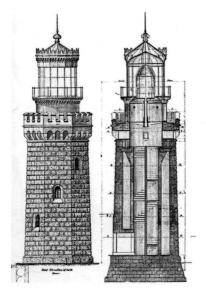

**From the plans for the 1862 north tower**

principal keeper and three assistants was the proper contingent.

The Lighthouse Board found some additional problems. The lanterns were too small to allow the keepers to easily do their work around the huge lenses, and several panes of lantern glass were broken. The lenses, although they were equal to the best in Europe at the time of their purchase, were by 1852 considered inferior to the lenses in newly constructed lighthouses in France, England, Scotland, and Ireland. Also, the condition of the towers was reported to be "very bad," with leaks and cracks.

The 1857 annual report of the Lighthouse Board stated that the towers were in a dilapidated condition, "the consequence of original bad materials and workmanship." There were fears that the buildings might not survive a severe winter storm.

In June 1860, Congress appropriated $72, 941 for the rebuilding of the station. Joseph Lederle was the architect who designed the new buildings, which look more like a medieval

castle than an American light station. The two castellated brownstone
towers were attached to each end of
an 18-room, 228-foot-long dwelling.
The south tower is square and the
north tower is octagonal, apparently
to make it easier for mariners to tell
them apart in the daytime.

The south tower was upgraded to
a fixed first-order lens at the time of
rebuilding in 1861–62, and the north
tower was given a new first-order
lens. In 1872, O. B. Bunce described
a visit to the light station in *Picturesque
America*:

> *A visit to this light-house will
> repay us; the view from the tower is
> superb, and the magnificent lenses of
> the lamp are well worth our curious
> attention. The obliging light-house
> keeper will draw the curtain, and
> show, reflected upon the convex cen-
> tral crystal, an exquisite miniature
> of all the expanse of land and sea
> and sky—such a landscape as the
> most gifted painter would despair of
> being able to imitate.*

In 1883, the lamp in the north
tower was converted from lard oil to
kerosene, marking the first time in
the nation that a first-order light was
fueled by kerosene. The south light
was converted to kerosene in the following year.

In January 1883, just before the
switch to kerosene, an assistant keeper
named Job Smith narrowly escaped
death in the south tower. The lard oil
was piped from a tank to the towers,
and in cold weather the oil often con-
gealed. Smith, who was alone at the
station, was holding an alcohol torch
to the pipe to heat the oil when the
alcohol holder became detached, and
the fluid poured in a burning stream
of fire onto his head.

Blinded with pain, Smith groped
his way down the tower stairs and
ran outside, engulfed in flames. He
fell into the deep snow and doused
the flames, but a newspaper reported
that his face and hands were "shock-
ingly burned." In spite of his wounds,
Smith continued with his work. He
climbed both towers and lighted both
lights for the night.

Keeper Murphy Rockette inspects the lens in the south tower.

In the morning, Smith signaled for assistance to the village below. The principal keeper arrived to relieve him, and Smith was taken to his home and given swift medical attention. It was reported that his wounds were not critical.

An interesting episode in the station's history took place in 1899, when Guglielmo Marconi conducted telegraphy experiments on the site. Gordon Bennett Jr., owner of the *New York Herald*, had invited Marconi to the site to report on the America's Cup sailboat race with his telegraph. An antenna was set up on top of the north lighthouse tower.

Before the race, Marconi's first telegraph transmissions in the United States had reported on the progress of Commodore George Dewey's fleet at the Battle of Manila Bay. Marconi maintained the wireless station for a time, but he eventually moved on to other locations that provided better reception.

From 1902 to 1907, the Navy Bureau of Equipment maintained a wireless station on the site. The facility was bought in 1907 by the Postal Telegraph Company, which attached the wireless station to a watchtower. A Postal Telegraph keeper reported on ships passing to and from New York Harbor.

The two lights remained fixed until 1898, when it was decided that the north light would be discontinued and the south tower would again have a flashing light with the addition of a new first-order bivalve Fresnel lens from Paris. The lens, manufactured by Henry Lepaute, had been displayed at the 1893 Columbian

Exposition in Chicago and was for a time intended for installation in Fire Island Light, New York.

A power plant built to supply electricity for the light was completed on June 30, 1898, and the new lens went into service, exhibiting a flash every five seconds. With an electric arc lamp inside the seven-ton lens, the south light became the most powerful lighthouse in the country at twenty-five million candlepower; there were reports of the light being seen seventy miles away when reflected off low clouds. The light in the north tower was extinguished on September 15, 1898.

The new light was so blindingly powerful that the keepers had to wear protective goggles if they entered the lantern room when the light was on. Not surprisingly, there were many complaints from neighbors about the light. It disturbed sleep and caused nervous afflictions, cows refused to give milk, and chickens stopped laying eggs. The Lighthouse Board took mercy, and some of the lantern panes on the landward side were darkened to shield the neighbors from the light.

By 1917, the electric generator was wearing out. Commercial electricity still wasn't available at the station, and the cost of replacing the generator was high. Officials instead decided to convert the light back to kerosene operation with the installation of an incandescent oil vapor lamp, then standard equipment in nonelectric lighthouses. The intensity of the light was lessened to 710,000 candlepower. The station

The north tower

was converted to commercial electricity in 1924, and the light got a boost back to 9,000,000 candlepower.

Among the station's longest serving keepers was Murphy Rockette, who arrived as a second assistant in 1921. Rockette was a native of North Carolina who served in both the army and navy before joining the Lighthouse Service. When Rockette and his eighteen-year-old wife, Elsie, moved into the station, it had no electricity or indoor plumbing. Water was obtained from a pump in the back yard.

The Rockettes stayed long enough to see the arrival of electricity, running water, and central heat. Rockette became the first assistant in 1928 and then rose to the rank of principal keeper in 1931. The Rockettes, who had one small child when they moved to the station, later welcomed a second daughter, born at the lighthouse.

The keepers at Navesink had the added responsibility of looking after many buoys in the nearby waters. The

The first-order Fresnel lens from the south tower is on display in the station's former power house.

Rockettes' daughter, Elsie Jane, later recalled that she preferred accompanying her father as he tended the buoys rather than cleaning her room. Elsie Jane's wedding reception was later held in the station's former power plant.

John Floherty wrote about Murphy Rockette in his 1942 book *Sentries of the Sea*. Floherty described the Rockette home as a "model of neatness and solid comfort" due to the "meticulous care and home interest of his capable wife."

In 1949, the 1898 lens was taken out of service; it was replaced by a smaller automated optic situated outside the lantern of the south tower. Rockette retired as the station's last keeper in 1951. The Rockettes were allowed to live at the station until 1952, when the light was discontinued.

The light station property was declared surplus property in 1953, and it was transferred to the Borough of Highlands in the following year. Soon, the Twin Lights Historical Society was formed to establish a museum. In 1962, the society began a partnership with the State of New Jersey. The New Jersey State Park Service, the Twin Lights Historical Society, and the Rumson Garden Club raised nearly a million dollars through donations and grants.

A major restoration of the property began in 1978. Lantern glass was replaced, the exterior stone and brickwork were repaired and cleaned, public restrooms were added, and the grounds were landscaped. Beginning in 1987, the exhibits in the museum were developed to focus on the history of the light station and lighthouse technology; there are also displays on the U.S. Life-Saving Service.

The 1898 first-order lens from the south tower is now on display in the former power house. The magnificent lens had been exhibited at the Boston Museum of Science from the 1950s until 1979.

The north tower now has a working navigational light, maintained by the New Jersey State Park Service. The museum at the Twin Lights

Historic Site, a national historic landmark, is open all year Wednesday through Sunday, 10:00 a.m. to 4:30 p.m. From Memorial Day to Labor Day, the museum is open seven days a week. The grounds are open every day, 9:00 a.m. to sunset. The north tower (sixty-four steps) is open for climbing when the museum is open. Group tours may be arranged in advance; call 732-872-1814.

To reach the site from North Jersey, take the Garden State Parkway South to exit 117 (Keyport/Hazlet) to Highway 36 South (East) and follow twelve miles to Highlands. Take the last right turn before the Highlands Bridge, which is Portland Road. Take a second immediate right turn onto Highland Avenue and continue past the condominiums on your left. The next intersection will be Lighthouse Road, (steep angle on left). Bear left onto Lighthouse Road and follow this road into the Twin Lights parking lot.

From South Jersey, take the Garden State Parkway North to exit 105 (Tinton Falls/Eatontown). Follow Highway 36 North (East) to Long Branch (also known as Joline Avenue). Highway 36 turns left onto Ocean Avenue and heads north. Go through the towns of Monmouth Beach and Seabright. Pass the entrance to Sandy Hook, Gateway National Recreation Area, and cross the Highlands Bridge. Take the first right turn off the bridge into Highlands; loop down under the bridge and up the other side of it. At the top of the hill, go straight onto Highland Avenue. The next intersection will be Lighthouse Road (steep angle on left). Bear left onto Lighthouse Road; follow this road into the Twin Lights parking lot.

For more information, contact the Twin Lights Historic Site, Lighthouse Road, Highlands, NJ 07732. Phone: 732-872-1814. Web site: www.twinlights.org.

# CONOVER BEACON

In August 1852, Congress appropriated funds for the establishment of a pair of range lights designed to help mariners negotiate the Chapel Hill Channel in Sandy Hook Bay. The channel connects the Ambrose Channel (the main route for shipping heading through the Narrows into New York Harbor) with the Sandy Hook Channel, which heads west to Raritan Bay.

**Accessibility:** 🚗

**Geographic coordinates:**
40° 25' 17" N   74° 03' 20" W

**Nearest community:**
Leonardo, New Jersey. Located on Sandy Hook Bay, on a beach in Leonardo.

**Established (Chapel Hill Range):** 1856. Present lighthouse built: 1926 (Originally stood in Keansburg as the front light in the Waackaack Range; moved to present site in 1941). Deactivated: 1988.

**Height of tower:** 45 feet.

Land for the rear light in the Chapel Hill neighborhood of Leonardo, New Jersey, was purchased from Timothy Mount. The front light took its name from Rulif Conover, who sold his land on the Leonardo waterfront to the government.

The front light was located about one and one-half miles north of the right light. The rear light originally was displayed from a fifty-five-foot-tall hexagonal wooden tower, built along with a wood-frame dwelling by Richard Calrow Jr. The range went into service in 1856.

The Chapel Hill Range was discontinued in 1923 after the channel was marked with gas-lighted buoys. This met with many complaints, so the range was soon reactivated and a single keeper was put in charge of both lights.

A cast-iron skeletal tower replaced the original rear tower in 1941. The skeletal tower was built in 1926, and it originally stood at Point Comfort in Keansburg, New Jersey, where it served as the front light of the Waackaack (pronounced "way-cake") Range. In its earlier location, it was known as Point Comfort Light and the Bayside Beacon.

The Chapel Hill Range was deactivated permanently in 1988, and the rear lighthouse was sold into private ownership; it remains a private home today. In 2004, ownership of the Conover Beacon was transferred to Monmouth County.

A preservation group, the Friends of Conover Beacon Society, was formed, but the beacon is still in dire need of restoration. For more on the preservation effort, call Dennis Robbins at 609-871-4425.

The Conover Beacon is on a beach near the intersection of Leonard Avenue and Beach Avenue in Leonardo, New Jersey.

## Fascinating Fact

This lighthouse was relocated in 1941; it originally stood at Point Comfort in Keansburg, New Jersey.

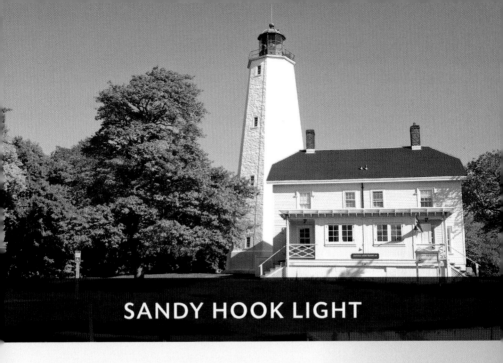

# SANDY HOOK LIGHT

On September 2, 1609, a lookout aboard Henry Hudson's vessel *Half Moon* spotted a "great fire" in the area we now know as the Highlands of Navesink, New Jersey. On the following day, some of the crew went ashore nearby at the low, sandy peninsula we now call Sandy Hook to attempt to barter with the local Indians. Things went well for a while, but when the Indians killed one of Hudson's men, the *Half Moon* pulled anchor and sailed up the river that now bears the explorer's name.

**Accessibility:**

**Geographic coordinates:**
40° 27' 39" N  73° 59' 49" W

**Nearest community:**
Fort Hancock (Middletown Township), New Jersey. Located near the northern tip of the Sandy Hook peninsula, on the approach to New York Harbor.

**Established:** 1764. Present lighthouse built: 1764. Automated: 1962.

**Height of tower:**
85 feet. Height of focal plane: 88 feet.

**Optic:** Third-order Fresnel lens.

**Characteristic:** Fixed white.

The seven-mile-long, 1,650-acre peninsula, in a vital position at the entrance to Lower New York Bay, was also known as Cedar Point; Dutch settlers dubbed it "Sandy Hoek."

The first known shipwreck at Sandy Hook was about 1620, when a Dutch vessel was cast ashore. The crew and passengers survived and walked to safety, except for a young man who had been injured and his eighteen-year-old bride, Penelope. The local Indians killed the young man, and his wife was badly wounded, but Penelope was nursed to health by one of the Indians and taken to the nearby Dutch settlement. She later married Richard Stout, and when Penelope Stout died at the age of 110, it was said that she had more than five hundred descendants.

## Fascinating Fact

This lighthouse, built in 1764, is the oldest standing lighthouse tower in the United States.

Richard Hartshorne, described as a "Quaker of a benevolent disposition," took up residence on the hills of Navesink in 1669, and he purchased from the natives an expansive tract of land that included all of Sandy Hook.

Ships traveling to New York Harbor used a natural channel that passed close to Sandy Hook. As early as 1679–80, Edmund Andros, the colonial governor of New York, suggested that the government buy Hartshorne's land for the purpose of erecting "seamarks for shipping" on Sandy Hook.

A warning beacon was established in the vicinity in 1746, but there were still no aids to navigation in 1755 when the Englishman Thomas Pownall sailed past Sandy Hook and described it as a "neck of low, sandy hills covered with cedar and holly." After passing Sandy Hook, Pownall wrote, the mariner "is delighted with the view of a most noble bay."

The peninsula's pleasing appearance belied its danger to mariners. In December 1757, a writer for the

*Pennsylvania Gazette,* reporting on a shipwreck, remarked, "It is surprising that a Light House has not been built long before this Day at Sandy Hook."

Six years after Pownall passed by, several additional shipwrecks occurred on the treacherous shoals and bars surrounding Sandy Hook. It was the financial losses from these wrecks that prompted forty-three local merchants to petition for a lighthouse.

The New York Assembly moved quickly, passing an act authorizing a lottery to raise a sum "not exceeding three thousand pounds" for the building of a lighthouse on Sandy Hook. A committee of four New York merchants was authorized to establish the lottery, which began on May 9, 1762. In the initial lottery, ten thousand tickets were sold at forty shillings each. More than sixteen hundred of

Undated view of Sandy Hook Lighthouse and keeper's house

the ticket buyers were prizewinners.

A week later, four acres of "barren, sandy soil" was purchased from Robert and Esek Hartshorne, for the "moderate price" of 750 pounds. The deed included some unusual provisions, including the "privilege of keeping and pasturing two cows on the lands" outside the tract that had been purchased and the agreement that "no public house for the selling of strong liquors" would be erected.

It took a second lottery in 1763 to raise enough funds for the completion

## SIDE TRIP: *Spermaceti Cove Visitor Center*

In spite of the lighthouses at Sandy Hook and the Navesink Highlands, shipwrecks in the vicinity were not uncommon. In 1848, a series of eight small huts was established on the shore from Sandy Hook to Long Beach and outfitted with rescue equipment and small boats. After the formation of the U.S. Life-Saving Service, a larger station was built at Spermaceti Cove two and one-half miles south of Sandy Hook Lighthouse in 1894. The restored building, classified as a Duluth-type station, now serves as the visitor center for the Sandy Hook unit of the Gateway National Recreation Area.

The visitor center, open from 10:00 a.m. to 5:00 p.m. daily, includes exhibits on the area and the history of lifesaving, a bookstore, and brochures to help you plan your visit. A self-guided nature tour begins at the station. Call the center for information on guided tours and special events.

**Spermaceti Cove Visitor Center**
**Gateway National Recreation Area**
**Sandy Hook Unit**
**P.O. Box 530**
**Fort Hancock, NJ 07732**
**Phone: 732-872-5970**
**Web site: www.nps/gov/gate/**

of the lighthouse, which was built about five hundred feet from the northern point of Sandy Hook. The *New York Mercury* announced on June 18, 1764:

> On Monday evening last, the
> NEW YORK LIGHT-HOUSE,
> erected at Sandy Hook, was lighted
> for the first time. The House is of an
> Octagon Figure, having eight equal
> sides; the Diameter at the Base, 29
> feet; and at the Top of the Wall, 15
> feet. The Lanthorn is 7 feet high; the
> Circumference 33 feet. The whole
> Construction of the Lanthorn is Iron;
> the top covered with Copper. There
> are 48 Oil Blazes. The Building
> from the Surface is Nine Stories;
> the whole from Bottom to Top, 103
> Feet. This structure was under-
> taken by Mr. Isaac Conro, of this
> City, and was carried on with all the
> Expedition that the Difficulty attend-
> ing to and fro on the Occasion that
> could possibly admit of; and is judged
> to be masterly finished.

Isaac Conro, the builder of the lighthouse, in addition to his work as a mason, was a New York merchant who dealt in building materials. Also involved in construction of the lantern was Robert Boyd, a blacksmith.

The New York Assembly authorized a tonnage tax of three pence per ton on all ships sailing into the harbor to pay for the upkeep of the stone lighthouse. In its first year, the tax raised 487 pounds.

Life at Sandy Hook was apparently quiet in the years before the American Revolution, except for a June 1766 lightning strike that broke lantern glass and did some damage to the keeper's house. It was reported that "some people that were in the House received a little Hurt, but are since recovered." The lightning was accompanied by "a heavy shower of Hail." A subsequent letter in the *New York Mercury* refuted the story, claiming that the presence of a lightning conductor on the tower had averted any damage.

In the early days of the Revolution, in March 1776, a small band of local patriots led by Major William Malcolm raided the lighthouse and removed the

The lighthouse tower at Sandy Hook is the oldest in the United States.

lamps and whale oil before the British fleet arrived. Malcolm was following orders to "render the lighthouse entirely useless" so it would serve no advantage for the British.

In June 1776, the lighthouse, while under the control of the British, was attacked by three hundred American troops under Lieutenant Colonel Benjamin Tupper. The *American Gazette* reported:

> *The enemy repaired to the Lighthouse, which was so strongly*

*fortified, and cemented, that the
shot from the field-pieces made no
impression, though not more than
150 yards distance; the Phoenix
and Liverpool, with springs on their
cables, poured in a heavy fire on our
men in flank and rear, while those at
the Light-house did the like in front,
for about two hours. The Colonel
finding his party somewhat fatigued,
and very much exposed to the fire
of the said ships, retired about two
miles to refresh his men.*

Their provisions nearly gone, the American troops left Sandy Hook that evening. The lighthouse remained under the control of the British through most of the Revolution. For a time, a refugee camp for Tories— known as the New Jersey Royal Volunteers or the "New Jersey Greens" after the color of their coats—was maintained around the lighthouse, and the refugee band made some attacks on its neighbors.

In late 1783, some British vessels were sent to remove the last British troops from New York and New Jersey. On New Year's Eve, six crewmen deserted the British man-of-war *Assistance,* anchored off Sandy Hook. Three officers and eleven crewmen were dispatched to apprehend the deserters, but the detachment's vessel was capsized as a snowstorm moved into the area, and all aboard were lost. The men were buried near the lighthouse; another crewman called the funeral a "most melancholy and awful procession."

In the early days of our nation, presidents took a personal interest in the management of lighthouses. One of George Washington's first official acts as president in August 1789 was to write a letter to the wardens of the Port of New York, directing them to keep the light burning until Congress could provide for its maintenance. In 1790, after the establishment of a federal lighthouse service, the light station was ceded to the federal government.

In 1796, the yearly salary of the keeper at Sandy Hook was $333.33. The names of the earliest keepers seem to have been lost to the passing years, but John Seaward was in charge in February 1790 when a sloop, the *Polly*, went aground at Sandy Hook on its way to New Haven, Connecticut.

Seaward was employed by the captain to help salvage materials from the wreck, and he was later able to refloat the vessel and take it to a local harbor. In April, the keeper had yet to be paid for his services, and he placed an ad in a local newspaper stating that the owners could have their vessel back if they paid him what he was owed, "or otherwise he will be under the necessity of taking such measures as the maritime laws of the state has provided in such cases."

A wooden beacon was erected near the lighthouse in 1790, as evidenced by a letter from Treasury Secretary Alexander Hamilton to President George Washington in June of that year: "The Secretary of the Treasury has the honor respectfully to submit to the President of the United States, for his approbation, the enclosed contract for timber, board,

## SIDE TRIP: *Fort Hancock*

This coastal defense fortification was established at the northern end of Sandy Hook in 1899. Thirty-four buildings were completed at that time, including eighteen homes for officers and their families. Many of the original structures remain.

The former post guardhouse, now known as the Fort Hancock Museum, contains exhibits on the fort and a bookstore. The museum is open 1:00 p.m. to 5:00 p.m. on weekends only April–November, and daily in July and August. History House, an 1898 lieutenant's residence along "Officers Row," is furnished as it was in the 1940s. The house is open weekends, 1:00 p.m. to 5:00 p.m. You can also tour Battery Potter, Sandy Hook's oldest gun battery (1893). Open weekends April–October, 1:00 p.m. to 4:00 p.m.

**Fort Hancock**
**Gateway National Recreation Area**
**Sandy Hook Unit**
**P.O. Box 530**
**Fort Hancock, NJ 07732**
**Phone: 732-872-5970**
**Web site: www.nps/gov/gate/**

Nails and workmanship, for a Beacon to be placed near the Light house on Sandy hook, the terms of which, he begs leave to observe are, in his opinion favorable to the U. States." The president approved the contract.

Two beacons had been built by March 1804, when a newspaper notice announced that the keeper had been instructed not to light the beacons "till further orders."

**Early 1900s**

In the early nineteenth century, the main lighthouse had a lighting system of eighteen whale oil lamps with eighteen-inch reflectors. By 1817, the keeper had the additional responsibility of caring for two additional navigational lights at Sandy Hook: the West Beacon and the East (North Hook) Beacon.

An 1838 inspection was critical of the east and west beacons, claiming that they were "too small and inadequate for their intentions." The beacons were rebuilt in 1842.

Stephen Pleasonton, the treasury official in charge of the nation's lighthouses, wrote in 1838 that the keeper, if unable to attend properly to all three lights, should hire an assistant; the keeper's yearly salary had been raised to $600 with that in mind. When the station was inspected in 1850, the keeper, John V. Canover (or Conover), was responsible for a total of thirty-two lamps in the lighthouse and the two additional beacons.

The 1850 inspection detailed some problems: "Lanterns of the lighthouses need painting, and the sashes want puttying or two or three coats of paint; either of them will probably make them tight. Found two of the lights in the main lantern cracked . . . The fence that encloses the light-house and dwelling is very much decayed . . ." The lighting apparatus in the east and west beacons was, however, deemed "first-rate."

With the formation of a new federal lighthouse board in 1852, the employment of a single keeper to attend all three lights was called into question. "The fact there is only one keeper at Sandy Hook, while there are five at Navesink, cannot fail to be remarked upon," read a report. "The lights are not lighted at sunsetting, and kept burning until sunrising, in compliance with instructions . . ."

It was pointed out that, to properly attend the lights, the keeper had to walk about three miles in the morning and evening, and it was impossible to attend to them properly during the night. The keeper at the time of the 1852 report, David Patterson, was paying for an assistant out of his own pocket. Finally, by 1857, Keeper Uriah Smalley was provided with three assistants.

The East Beacon, a thirty-five-foot-tall wooden tower, was fitted with a fifth-order Fresnel lens in 1855, and the West Beacon, also thirty-five feet tall, received a sixth-order lens in 1856.

A third-order Fresnel lens replaced the system of multiple lamps and reflectors in the main lighthouse in 1857, and the lens remains in service today. Also in 1857, a brick lining was added to the tower along with iron stairs and floors.

The East Beacon was rebuilt in 1867, with a tower attached to a wood-frame dwelling. Just two months after it went into service, the building was destroyed by fire. It was soon rebuilt. An important experiment was conducted at the East Beacon in 1868, when the nation's first fog siren was installed. An 1869 storm caused great damage, and the beacon was again rebuilt in 1870, 500 feet to the south.

As the East Beacon was threatened by erosion, it was replaced in 1880 by a cast-iron tower farther back from the shore. At this time, the beacon became known as the North Beacon or North Hook Beacon. In 1889, it became one of the first lighthouses in the United States to be powered by electricity; electric power was extended to the main light in 1896. The cast-iron tower was later relocated to Jeffrey's Hook on Manhattan, where it still stands, beloved as the Little Red Lighthouse. An automated light on a skeletal tower serves as the North Beacon today.

The West Beacon fought a long battle with erosion. Jetties added in 1867 to protect the beacon weren't enough; the structure had to be put on oak piles driven deep into the sand. Then, in 1889, the beacon was moved 440 feet to the south, where it served as a range light with the main lighthouse. From this time, it was known as the South Beacon.

According to the historian Edward Rowe Snow in his book *Famous Lighthouses of America*, sometime in the mid-1800s, the keepers' dwelling by the main lighthouse had no visible entrance to the basement. One keeper managed to loosen some floorboards, allowing him access to the basement.

"A moment later," wrote Snow, "he was horrified to discover a skeleton propped up at a table, facing what was apparently a rude fireplace." There has been no documentation

A look inside Sandy Hook's third-order Fresnel lens

to prove or disprove this story. A new two-and-one-half-story, duplex wood-frame keepers' house was constructed in 1883, replacing the "old and dilapidated stone dwelling."

Since the late 1890s, Sandy Hook Lighthouse has stood alongside the buildings of Fort Hancock. Like most American lighthouses, the light was extinguished during both world wars. During World War II, the tower was painted in a camouflage pattern to hide it from possible enemy attack.

Another rare extinguishing of the light took place during a tremendous storm in August 1933. The same storm dragged the Diamond Shoals Lightship in North Carolina five miles off its station and did great damage to York Spit Light Station in Chesapeake Bay. At Sandy Hook, the electric power lines were knocked down about 6:30 p.m., but an auxiliary oil-powered light was put into service after about an hour.

Edward Rowe Snow, in his role as the "Flying Santa" to lighthouse keepers and their families, twice landed at Sandy Hook to bring gifts just before Christmas. He described his 1948 visit: "I climbed the venerable lighthouse steps with Keeper Richard Terhune, and we looked out over Sandy Hook and the ocean that afternoon, each of us thinking of the vast amount of shipping which has passed and which will pass the ancient lighthouse in the years to come."

The light was automated in 1962. In 1964, on its 200th birthday, Sandy Hook Lighthouse was designated a National Historic Landmark. Today, after so many years of shifting sands at Sandy Hook, the lighthouse stands more than a mile from the northern tip of the peninsula. Both the lighthouse and Fort Hancock are part of the Gateway National Recreation Area.

In 1996, ownership of the lighthouse passed from the Coast Guard to the National Park Service. The Coast Guard continues to maintain the lighting apparatus and related equipment. A $650,000 restoration was completed in 2000, leaving the tower in its best condition in many years. The Sandy

Hook Foundation, the park's friends group, funded the work.

The keepers' house now serves as a visitor center and as headquarters for the New Jersey Lighthouse Society and the Sandy Hook Foundation. The New Jersey Lighthouse Society partners with the National Park Service in the interpretation of the lighthouse.

Tours of America's oldest lighthouse tower are offered on a first-come, first-served basis. Visitors must be at least forty-eight inches tall to climb the tower. Groups need reservations in advance for a lighthouse tour; contact the park visitor center at 732-872-5970. Tours are given on weekends from noon to 4:30 p.m. from April to early December. From April to October, tours are also given on weekdays from 1:30 to 4:30 p.m.

To reach the lighthouse from northern New Jersey and New York, travel south on the New Jersey Turnpike and take exit 11 onto the Garden State Parkway South. Take exit 117 (Keyport/Hazlet). After the toll, bear left and follow Route 36 East for twelve miles to the Gateway National Recreation Area/Sandy Hook entrance.

From southern New Jersey, travel north on the Garden State Parkway and take exit 105 (Eatontown). Bear left onto Route 36 East across Route 35 through Eatontown and Long Branch. Continue on Route 36, which turns left and follows north along the shore. Continue north for six miles through the towns of Long Branch, Monmouth Beach, and Sea Bright to the Gateway National Recreation Area/Sandy Hook.

From Philadelphia and Camden, New Jersey, follow the New Jersey Turnpike north to exit 7A (Shore Points) onto I-195. Follow east to the Garden State Parkway North. Follow to exit 105 (Eatontown), and then follow the "From southern New Jersey" directions above.

For more information, visit www.nps/gov/gate/ online or call 732-872-5970.

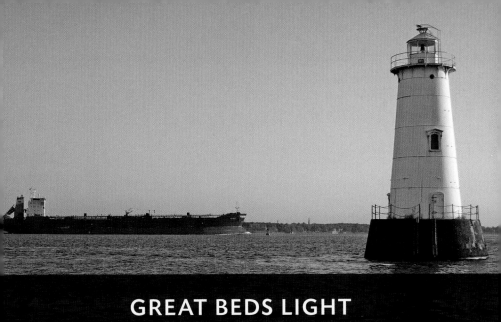

# GREAT BEDS LIGHT

It's historically listed as a New York lighthouse, but this cast-iron tower clearly stands a few feet on the New Jersey side of the border at the mouth of the Raritan River between South Amboy, New Jersey, and Staten Island, New York. It's about three-quarters of a mile south of Ward Point on Staten Island.

**Accessibility:** 🏛⛵

**Geographic coordinates:**
40° 29' 12" N   74° 15' 11" W

**Nearest community:** South Amboy, New Jersey. Located in Raritan Bay near the mouth of the Raritan River.

**Established:** 1880. Present lighthouse built: 1880. Automated: 1945.

**Height of tower:** 60 feet. Height of focal plane: 61 feet.

**Previous optic:** Fourth-order Fresnel lens. Present optic: 155 mm.

**Characteristic:** Red flash every 6 seconds.

The name "Great Beds" comes from the area's rich oyster beds. The name was used at least as early as 1719, when the New Jersey colonial assembly passed a law decreeing that "No gathering oysters from the [New Jersey] half of the Great Beds should take place between May tenth and September first and none of its oysters should be taken by any vessel not owned within New Jersey."

Mariners petitioned for a lighthouse in the vicinity in 1868, and the Lighthouse Board deemed the request reasonable. The 1869 annual report of the Lighthouse Board noted, "The attention of Congress is again invited to the subject," but it would take several more years before action was taken. In 1878, the Lighthouse Board announced:

> *The advisability of erecting a light-house at this point was recently made the subject of a report to the Secretary of the Treasury. The point which would most fully meet the wants of navigation and commerce is on the shoal head or junction of the channels of the Raritan River and the Kill Von Kull, about one-third of a mile off the south end of Staten Island, in 5 feet depth at low water.*

Congress appropriated $34,000 for the lighthouse in June 1878. By the following year, the State of New Jersey ceded the site to the federal government and work began. Before the actual construction began, it was determined that the lighthouse should be built about a quarter-mile south of the site originally specified. It was then realized that the State of New York had jurisdiction over both sites according to an 1834 agreement, and work was suspended until the next assembling of the New York legislature.

In April 1880, the State of New York ceded the site to the United

## Fascinating Fact

Raritan Bay was so solidly frozen in early 1918 that people drove their automobiles around the lighthouse, about a mile offshore.

States. Work on the pier and lighthouse superstructure swiftly progressed. During construction, a retired wooden lightship, the *LV-15*, served as quarters for the workmen.

The light went into service on November 15, 1880, with a fourth-order Fresnel lens showing a fixed red light fifty-seven feet above mean high water. In June 1898, a 1,227-pound fog bell was added, with machinery striking a double blow every fifteen seconds. The first keeper was David C. Johnson.

In April 1883, the *New York Times* reported that the keeper, George Brennen, had been missing for several days. Brennen had gone to the custom house in Perth Amboy to pick up his pay and then accompanied friends to South Amboy. He started back in his rowboat for the lighthouse early in the evening, but residents on shore noticed that the light wasn't lit that night.

The keeper's overturned boat washed up on the beach the next morning. It was reported that he was

Early 1900s view

"of sober habits," and the reason for the capsizing of the boat wasn't clear. Brennen's body was eventually found.

Just four months later, on August 28, 1883, the *New York Times* reported that Brennen's replacement, John E. Johnson, had been missing for ten days. He had last been seen on duty at the lighthouse on August 18, and his boat was found moored at the station. His coat was in the boat, and his keys were inside the lighthouse on a table. Some speculated that Johnson had committed suicide, while others thought that the keeper, who had a wife and four children, "disappeared for a reason."

David J. Johnson, a Civil War veteran who was a relative of the first keeper, took over as principal keeper in 1894. Johnson lost his job four years later over a dispute with the assistant keeper, John Anderson. It seems that Johnson's family was living at the lighthouse and consuming government rations without permission. Anderson was also dismissed for using "indecent language" in the presence of Johnson's family.

Vessels collided with the lighthouse with frightening regularity, with an average of about one collision per year in the early 1900s. On January 25, 1906, Keeper John Osterdahl was on an early morning watch when a line of barges being towed by a tug smashed into the lighthouse. Luckily, the damage was slight, and the towing company picked up the $20 tab for damage to the station's ladder.

In 1916, the keeper, Ellsworth J. Smith, after spending many lonely hours at the lighthouse, placed an ad for a wife in a local newspaper. The ad ran for three months before Helen Barry of New Haven, Connecticut, replied. Preparations began, but when Ms. Barry admitted she was only sixteen years old, the city clerk in Perth Amboy refused to grant a license. A newspaper reported that Smith was "steeped in gloom" but that he was determined "to find a wife yet."

In unusually cold winters, the waters of Raritan Bay sometimes froze solid. It was reported in January 1918 that at least four automobiles drove out around the lighthouse and back to South Amboy. Two men reportedly enjoyed a game of golf on the frozen bay.

On October 4, 1918, a series of accidental explosions began at a munitions plant in Morgan, New Jersey. The first explosion was so great that the lighthouse shook and three panes of lantern glass were shattered. Throughout the night, several ensuing shocks caused the light to go out. The keeper spent the night in the lantern, keeping the light going through extraordinary circumstances.

The light was automated and destaffed in 1945. The still-operating lighthouse is depicted on the city seal of South Amboy, and it was added to the National Register of Historic Places in 2008.

The lighthouse may be seen distantly from Raritan Bay Maritime Park in South Amboy. Take the Garden State Parkway to exit 124, turn east toward South Amboy on Main Street (in Sayerville). Go straight at the first light onto Washington Avenue. Continue to a stop sign and turn left onto Main Street (in South Amboy). Continue east on Main Street to the second light and turn right on Broadway. Continue south on Broadway for seven blocks to John Street. Turn left on John Street, crossing the railroad tracks, and turn right at the stop sign onto Roswell Street, which soon becomes John T. O'Leary Boulevard. Continue to the entrance to the park on your left just before you reach another railroad crossing. The park road ends in a circle next to the bay, and there is ample free parking.

There's also a distant view available from Conference House Park on Staten Island, New York. Take Hyland Boulevard on Staten Island to its southern end and turn right onto Saterlee Street. The park and beach will be on your left.

For a much closer look, you may charter a cruise with Ray Mellett of Sewaren; call 973-953-7781.

Great Beds Light surrounded by ice in the early 1900s

# ROMER SHOAL LIGHT

**Accessibility:** 🏚 ⛵

**Geographic coordinates:**
40° 30' 49" N   74° 00' 48" W

**Nearest community:**
Borough of Staten Island,
New York. Located in New
Jersey waters about two
miles north of Sandy Hook
and about 2.5 miles south of
Staten Island.

**Established:** 1886 (skeletal
tower). Present lighthouse
built: 1898. Automated:
1966.

**Height of tower:**
54 feet. Height of focal
plane: 54 feet.

**Previous optic:** Fourth-
order Fresnel lens (1898).
Present optic: 190 mm.

**Characteristic:** Two white
flashes every 15 seconds.

**Fog signal:** Horn, two blasts
every 15 seconds.

Romer Shoal, about two miles north of Sandy Hook, is named for Colonel Wolfgang William Römer, a British military engineer who charted the local waters around 1700. A spar buoy marked the southwest part of the shoal as early as 1825.

Early 1900s view

In November 1837, the Treasury Department announced that a "skillful engineer" had been employed to examine the shoal, which was a dangerous obstruction in the Swash Channel, and to furnish a plan for a beacon on the shoal. At a cost of $25,000, a conical granite day beacon was erected in 1838. A wooden mast and a square wooden cage daymark surmounted the twenty-five-foot-tall beacon.

The site selected by Winslow Lewis at the northwestern end of the shoal turned out to be about a mile from the correct position. It was at the wrong end of the shoal, meaning the beacon did not serve as a guide for the Swash Channel. Still, it did serve to warn mariners of the shallow area. Mariners were warned not to "run for the beacon, or they would infallibly get on shore."

By 1870, the east side of the beacon's foundation had been undermined by the sea, and the structure had settled. A sum of $5,000 was appropriated for repairs in 1871, and nearly a thousand tons of granite

**Fascinating Fact**

A skeletal tower that stood on this site from 1886 to 1898 was one of the nation's first lighthouses to be fueled by acetylene gas.

blocks were piled around the foundation for protection. By 1877, the beacon had settled to one side; more riprap protection was added after an additional appropriation of $5,000.

By 1883, mariners petitioned for a proper lighthouse on the shoal, as vessels continued to run aground with regularity. The Lighthouse Board proclaimed that the building of a lighthouse on the shoal was "impracticable" and that a light would instead be added to the existing day beacon and be lighted with gas.

The authorities soon decided that a new structure in a more advantageous location was needed. In 1886, a new skeletal tower on an iron pier was constructed at the opposite end of the shoal at a cost of $14,336. Arnold

Burges Johnson's 1889 book *The Modern Light-House Service*, provides a description:

> The structure is on an iron pier, 30 feet in diameter and 16 feet high, surmounted by an iron skeleton tower 25 feet high, from which is shown a fixed white fifth-order light, the focal plane of which is 41 feet above mean low water, and which should be seen some 11 miles. It was first lighted on the night of July 15, 1886. It is lighted with compressed gas from a tank which holds about a ninety-days' supply.

Johnson pointed out that the cost of the structure was far less than that of a lighthouse and that the maintenance costs were relatively low. Over the next decade, however, the equipment proved unreliable. A proper lighthouse was finally built on the site in 1898.

The new fifty-four-foot-tall, cast-iron lighthouse, with a fourth-order Fresnel lens showing a flashing white light, went into service on October 1, 1898. Before it was assembled on the shoal, the superstructure had been used for experimental purposes at the lighthouse depot on Staten Island. The station included a 1,300-pound fog bell, struck by machinery every thirty seconds.

Even with the improved lighthouse and fog signal, wrecks on the shoal were not uncommon. In September 1899, the schooner *Penokee*,

Before it was assembled at Romer Shoal, the lighthouse superstructure stood at a lighthouse depot on Staten Island.

heading from Norfolk, Virginia, to Saco, Maine, with a cargo of coal, went aground while seeking shelter in a gale. The crew of seven managed to escape in a lifeboat to the lifesaving station at Sandy Hook, but the vessel was a total loss.

Another in a long line of accidents on the shoal occurred in early June 1905, when the Gloucester fishing schooner *James Drinan* went ashore while on route to New York Harbor with a cargo of mackerel. The crew of a passing schooner rescued the eight men on board, while the *Drinan* was pounded to pieces by the heavy seas.

The tower was a males-only "stag" station with accommodations for three keepers. In May 1919, six U.S. Navy signal quartermasters were assigned to the lighthouse to keep an eye on the passing maritime traffic; the men moved in with the three Lighthouse Service keepers. The conditions must have been unbearably crowded, and the six men were mercifully reassigned after a few weeks.

The lighthouse remained in navy control until October 1921. Tragedy struck in November 1920, when Quartermaster William Walker went out in the station's small boat to meet a larger vessel that was delivering provisions. As the larger vessel turned, Walker's boat was swamped by the wake from the propeller, and the sailor was drowned.

An even greater disaster occurred in September 1935. The lighthouse tender *Tulip* was bringing construction supplies to the lighthouse in choppy seas. The tender could only get within about 300 feet of the lighthouse, so a smaller workboat was used to transfer the supplies. As a group of ten men prepared to unload more materials, another group of ten was on route to the lighthouse in the workboat.

Suddenly, the men working on the tender were alerted by the cries of two young mess boys, who shouted that the workboat had capsized about halfway to the lighthouse, and the men were struggling in the water. The boat had been overturned when it was broadsided by a large wave.

Henry O. Austin, the captain of the tender, ordered the immediate launch of a lifeboat. Under the command of Ignors Bolstatch, the lifeboat made it to the capsized workboat. By the time the lifeboat arrived, several of the men had already disappeared in the heavy seas, and the others were exhausted.

Romer Shoal Light in October 2008

Six men, including one who was unconscious, were pulled into the lifeboat. The unconscious man later died. Five men died in the accident, but five others were saved, thanks to the quick action of the other crewmen from the *Tulip*.

Herman Westgate, who had been in charge for a decade, was the principal keeper when the devastating hurricane of 1938 struck. The hurricane did its worst damage along the south coast of New England, where more than 700 people died. Westgate reported that the water around the lighthouse looked black during the hurricane. Luckily, the damage to the structure was minor, and Westgate survived without injury.

During the Coast Guard era beginning in 1939, four men were assigned to the station with three at the lighthouse at all times. A 1949 article in the *New York Times* profiled the crewmen, whose average age was twenty-two. The officer in charge was twenty-nine-year-old Boatswain's Mate Third Class Sven Espenbaum.

The men were awarded six days of liberty after each twenty-four-day stint at the lighthouse.

The day began at 7:00 a.m. with the checking of the generators and the compressors for the foghorn. In good weather, the men cleaned and painted the lighthouse and their boats. Once a week, a crewman went by motorboat to Midland Beach on Staten Island to pick up mail and groceries. Visitors were rare, other than the occasional pigeons that would land and spend the night.

"It's a nice, quiet life," said twenty-two-year-old Engineman Third Class Jerry Confessore of Brooklyn, New York. "We're on duty eight hours a day and then pull a four-hour duty trick at night. The rest of the time we've got to ourselves. I can read up on mechanics and help advance my rating. And I don't feel very far from Ebbets Field. We've got a television set, and I can watch all the Brooklyn games."

Seaman Apprentice Edward DeWaine, nineteen years old, said he felt lonesome at times and planned to bring his beagle, Snuffy, to the lighthouse for company. Seventeen-year-old Seaman Apprentice Charles Alair stayed busy in his spare time by working on a canvas table cover, edged with tassels.

The station was automated and destaffed in 1966. A storm in December 1992 damaged the structure, and the Coast Guard briefly considered replacing it with a simple steel tower. Repairs were completed instead, thanks largely to the advocacy of Staten Island resident Joseph Esposito, and the lighthouse has survived in reasonably good condition to the present day.

Romer Shoal Lighthouse may be seen distantly from the northernmost part of the Sandy Hook peninsula, but it's best seen by boat. For a close look, you may charter a cruise with Ray Mellett of Sewaren, New Jersey; call 973-953-7781.

# OLD ORCHARD SHOAL LIGHT

**Accessibility:** 🏛️ ⚓

**Geographic coordinates:**
40° 30' 45" N   74° 05' 56" W

**Nearest community:**
Borough of Staten Island,
New York. Located offshore
about two miles southeast of
Great Kills Harbor.

**Established:** 1893. Present
lighthouse built: 1893.
Automated: 1955.

**Height of tower:**
45 feet. Height of focal
plane: 51 feet.

**Previous optic:** Fourth-
order Fresnel lens (1893).
Present optic: 250 mm.

**Characteristic:** White flash
every 6 seconds, with two
red sectors.

West Bank and Old Orchard Shoal,
parts of the dangerous Staten
Island Flats extending from the southeast
part of Staten Island, form a border on
the main channel into New York Harbor.
In 1890, the Lighthouse Board made the
following plea for funds to erect a lighthouse at Old Orchard Shoal, located
about two miles southeast of Great Kills
Harbor on Staten Island:

*When the sound is closed by ice, it is stated that 15,000 tons of shipping per day pass through this bay. All this shipping would be benefited by the establishment of a light and fog-signal at this point. The large tows approaching Orchard Shoal are obliged to hug the shore of Staten Island as closely as possible, and they use the inner channel between the west bank and Staten Island. The channel is quite narrow.*

A lighted gas buoy, a bell buoy, and a spar buoy already marked the shoal, but something more substantial was needed. It was proposed that the new lighthouse would form a range with the Waackaack Light in Keansburg, New Jersey.

The 1855 Waackaack Light, a hexagonal wooden tower with a focal plane height of seventy-six feet, was too short to serve adequately as a rear range light. A congressional appropriation of $60,000 in March 1891 was intended to pay for the rebuilding of that tower, along with the

## Fascinating Fact

This lighthouse was sold via online auction in 2008 for a high bid of $235,000.

construction of a new lighthouse at Old Orchard Shoal.

Work was well underway at both sites during 1892, but the project ran into a snag that put it over budget. The price for the removal of the old Waackaack tower had been underestimated, and a new tariff act meant that duties totaling $1,300 were due on the lenses for the two locations. After an additional appropriation of $4,030, work proceeded.

The cast-iron caisson lighthouse at Old Orchard Shoal went into service on April 25, 1893, with a fourth-order Fresnel lens showing an occulting white light. A fog siren, operated by an oil engine, was added in 1897.

A new skeletal tower in Keansburg displayed two lights at different heights; the upper light served as a rear range with the Point Comfort

Keansburg Light, Keansburg, N. J.

**This 106-foot skeletal tower served as the Waackacck Rear Range Light beginning in 1894.**

exhaustion" in 1902. His worries had probably been exacerbated when the light was extinguished for reasons of security during the Spanish-American War from April to August 1898. Adolph Nordstrom succeeded Carlow as keeper.

Boating mishaps near the lighthouse were common. In 1914 alone, the principal keeper, Edward M. Grant, was recognized twice by the Department of Commerce for going to the aid of boaters in trouble. On the first occasion, he saved the occupants of a disabled powerboat "at great risk" and repaired the engine so the party could continue on their way. Later that year, he went to the aid of a boat disabled about three-quarters of a mile from the lighthouse. It was reported that he towed the boat to the lighthouse and gave the occupants "breakfast and dinner."

Light about three-quarters of a mile away. The lower light served as a rear range with the Old Orchard Shoal Light offshore, marking the line of best water between Staten Island and West Bank.

Old Orchard Shoal's first keeper was Alfred L. Carlow, a former lightship sailor. Carlow apparently found life at the isolated lighthouse even more stressful than lightship duty; he was hospitalized for "nervous

Andrew Zuius, formerly at Sakonnet Point Light in Rhode Island, was the keeper in June 1927, when a motorboat developed a leak near the lighthouse during a storm. Zuius rushed to the aid of the four men on board as their boat was almost completely underwater, and he got them safely to the lighthouse where he provided them with food and shelter.

One of the light's keepers around 1940 was Frank Schubert, who spent three years at Old Orchard Shoal before a long stretch at Coney Island Light. Schubert later told author Jim Crowley that the hardest part of life at the "sparkplug" light was the cramped living quarters, which often caused keepers to get on each other's nerves toward the end of their twenty-one-day tours.

Much of the keepers' spare time was occupied with fishing and lobstering with homemade traps. During Schubert's time, the keepers would occasionally go ashore in a small skiff at Miller Field, Staten Island, to pick up their mail and supplies, leaving one keeper in charge at the lighthouse.

The long, quiet stretches at Old Orchard Shoal led Schubert to take up a lifelong hobby—marquetry, which is defined as the "coverage of the entire surface of a board or piece of furniture with veneer, in the form of a skillfully applied design or picture." Schubert became an accomplished practitioner of this art.

The lighthouse was automated in 1955, and the last Coast Guard keepers were reassigned. The range with the Waackaack beacon was discontinued many years ago, but Old Orchard Shoal Light continues as an automated aid to navigation.

In 2007, under the provisions of the National Historic Lighthouse Preservation Act of 2000, the lighthouse was made available to a suitable new steward. There were no applicants, so the property was offered to the general public via online auction in August 2008. The high bid was $235,000. Luckily for the private owners, the station's fog signal is no longer active.

Old Orchard Shoal Light may be seen very distantly from the beach at Great Kills Park on Staten Island. For a much better look, you can charter a cruise with Ray Mellett of Sewaren, New Jersey; call 973-953-7781.

# PRINCE'S BAY LIGHT

**Geographic coordinates:**
40° 30' 28" N   74° 12' 48" W

**Nearest community:**
Borough of Staten Island,
New York. Located on a
high bluff at the Mt. Loretto
Unique Area, south coast of
Staten Island.

**Established:** 1828. Present
lighthouse built: 1864.
Deactivated: 1922.

**Height of tower:** 40 feet.

**Previous optic:** Three-and-
one-half-order Fresnel lens
(1857). Fourth-order Fresnel
lens (1890).

Prince's Bay, also known as Princess Bay, is a small indentation on the south coast of Staten Island. According to local legend, the bay, which was long famous for its rich oyster beds, was named for a prince who often feasted on oysters for their aphrodisiac qualities.

Keeper John Anderson at
Princes Bay Light, circa 1917,
with his wife, Hannah, and their
dog, Snooks

The bluffs that border the bay rise about eighty feet from the water and are the highest seaside cliffs in the state of New York. The location where the lighthouse stands has also been known as Red Bank and Lighthouse Hill.

Congress appropriated $30,000 in May 1826 for three light stations: on the Highlands of Navesink in New Jersey, near Fort Tompkins on Staten Island, and at Prince's Bay. A thirty-foot-tall rubblestone tower, with its fixed white light 106 feet above the water, was completed in 1828.

The lighthouse's eleven lamps and reflectors were positioned so that they served shipping traffic coming from the southwest, headed north to New York Harbor. In 1837, three local captains suggested that the placing of additional reflectors would be of great value to local traffic. Suitable alterations were soon completed.

Silas Bidell became keeper in July 1849. An 1850 inspection report described him as "new and inexperienced." Like other inexperienced

**Fascinating Fact**

The bluffs in the vicinity of this lighthouse are the highest seaside cliffs in the state of New York.

keepers, the report continued, Bidell was "a great consumer of oil." The buildings needed whitewashing, and the fences needed repair; the report concluded, "Keeper is nothing extra." An 1851 report was no kinder. The keeper "was ignorant of his duties, and evidently not aware of the importance of keeping a good light." Bidell made no written reports and often left the station, sometimes leaving his daughter in charge. Homer Phelps succeeded Bidell as keeper about a year later.

In November 1857, a three-and-one-half-order Fresnel lens replaced the old system of multiple lamps and reflectors. At the same time, the light was changed to fixed white with a more brilliant flash every two minutes. This change was designed to prevent mariners from confusing the light with several other lights in the vicinity of Staten Island. In 1890, a new fourth-order lens was installed, showing a flashing white light.

By 1863, the original tower was in poor condition. A new brownstone tower, forty feet tall, was completed in 1864. The original dwelling was destroyed in 1868, when a new two-and-one-half-story brownstone keeper's house was completed and attached to the tower by a short passageway. The materials from the old house were used to build a new barn.

Erosion of the bank where the lighthouse stood was quickened by heavy rains, and a $12,000 appropriation in 1870 paid for added protection in the form of a sea wall. The contractor who built the wall lost a barge during the storm, slowing progress. The wall was completed, along with new jetties on the beach below the lighthouse site, by 1874. The wall had given way in several places by 1879, and another appropriation of $3,500 was needed to strengthen it.

With the establishment of new automatic acetylene-powered lights in the vicinity, the authorities decided in 1922 that the Prince's Bay Light was no longer needed. It was deactivated on August 31, 1922, and the lantern was removed.

The lighthouse reservation was bordered by the Mission of the Immaculate Virgin, an orphanage and school. The mission purchased the lighthouse property

**Early 1900s view**

at auction in 1926. The keeper's house was used as a residence for the mission's directors until 1988, and Cardinal John J. O'Connor sometimes used it for retreats. During this period, the mission placed a statue of the Virgin Mary atop the lanternless lighthouse tower. The statue has been removed in recent years.

The lighthouse property and 145 adjoining acres were purchased by the State of New York in 1999. The New York State Department of Environmental Conservation manages the property, now known as the Mt. Loretto Unique Area. In recent years, a rear range light on a small steel tower has been erected near the lighthouse. A skeletal tower on lower ground holds the front light for the Prince's Bay Range.

The area immediately around the lighthouse and keeper's house is encompassed by a fence and is not accessible to the public. Because of the high trees, the lighthouse cannot be seen from the water or from the nearby beach.

On Staten Island, park in the small parking area for the Mt. Loretto Unique Area, at 6450 Hylan Boulevard. On I-278, take the exit for 440 South (West Shore Expressway). Take the last exit (# 1) on 440 South. At the end of the ramp, turn right at the traffic light. At the next intersection, take another right. At the traffic light, make a third right. This puts you on Page Avenue. Follow Page through four traffic lights, and then turn left onto Hylan Boulevard. The parking lot for Mt. Loretto will be about three-quarters of a mile along Hylan, on the right side.

Follow the trail from the parking area to its end, turn left, and follow to the lighthouse property. During much of the year, the surrounding trees hide the lighthouse from view, but the keeper's house can be seen.

For more information on the Mt. Loretto Unique Area, visit www.dec. ny.gov/outdoor/8291.html online, call 718-482-6404, or e-mail mtlorett@ gw.dec.state.ny.us.

# WEST BANK LIGHT

**Accessibility:** 🏚 ⚓

**Geographic coordinates:**
40° 30' 28" N   74° 12' 48" W

**Nearest community:**
Borough of Staten Island,
New York. Located about
two and one-half miles off
South Beach on Staten Island.

**Established:** 1901. Present
lighthouse built: 1901.
Automated: 1985.

**Height of tower:**
55 feet. Height of focal
plane: 79 feet.

**Previous optic:** Fourth-
order Fresnel lens (1901).

**Characteristic:** Red light
to the east, white to the
west; three seconds on, three
seconds off.

As the work of improving the main ship channels into New York Harbor progressed in the late nineteenth century, the Lighthouse Board in 1896 proposed a lighthouse on West Bank, off Staten Island in the lower bay. The board asked for an appropriation of $50,000, and Congress complied in June 1897.

**Early 1900s view**

The exact site for the lighthouse wasn't determined until 1900, and work began that summer. In July, the shoal was excavated to a depth of eight to ten feet below the bottom. A 380,000-pound foundation cylinder was sunk into position and filled with concrete. The foundation was completed in November, and the work of erecting the lighthouse superstructure began. The project was completed in December, and the light went into service on January 1, 1901, with a fourth-order Fresnel lens showing a fixed white light with a red sector. A fog siren was established in June 1901.

The new lighthouse nearly met a premature demise on December 28, 1904. A large ship, being towed by a tugboat, crashed into the tower, ripping away railings and breaking glass. The towing company paid for the $1,200 in damages. Ed Burge, the principal keeper, was in the lighthouse at the time. In an interview years later, he said, "She tore out one side of the tower, ripped free and drifted on, leaving that gale pouring through

**Fascinating Fact**

This was the last lighthouse in the Third District to be automated, in 1985. It was sold at auction in 2008 for a high bid of $245,000.

my bedroom. Nope, I didn't do anything heroic. A man can't be much of a hero without his pants."

Less than a year later, another collision caused damage to the foundation caisson. After more than a decade of additional deterioration, the foundation was repaired in July 1916, at a cost of almost $11,000. A protective riprap bulkhead was created around the base of the lighthouse.

Many people have romantic notions about the life of a lighthouse keeper, and Ed Burge was quick to dispel such thoughts in a 1924 interview:

*I met a lady once who was all filled up with what she called the romance of the lighthouse. She said she often longed to be a keeper and live alone in a tower on a rock far out in the sea, and have peace and quiet. Peace and quiet! A lighthouse is about the noisiest place in the world. Out there on West Bank, for instance, with a gale blowing. When I was there, the tower rose right out of the water, with no footing at all around it, so the waves crashed against the whole tower; shook it until sometimes the mantles over the burners in the light broke. Sometimes the waves went clear over the gallery, and the spray over the light itself . . . . Nice, romantic spot - so quiet that the keeper can scarcely hear the whistles of steamers and tugs in the channel.*

In January 1908, the height of the tower was increased with the addition of two stories below the watch room, at a cost of about $9,000. In 1912, the higher light became a front range light in tandem with the new lighthouse at Richmond Hill on Staten Island. The range helped guide mariners through the important Ambrose Channel.

In early January 1908, when the work of raising the tower was nearly complete, two vessels of the North Atlantic Fleet, the *Kentucky* and the *Kearsarge*, collided near the lighthouse. Damage to the ships was significant, but there were no injuries.

During bitterly cold weather in

---

## SIDE TRIP: *Staten Island's South Beach*

One of Staten Island's most popular attractions, South Beach offers free concerts and fireworks in summer. At the northern end of the restored boardwalk, nearly two miles long, is the spectacular Dolphin Fountain, an iconic structure for Staten Islanders. At the southern end is Freedom Circle, which pays special tribute to the women and men of the armed forces. Freedom Circle displays American flags from six important moments in our history as well as educational displays about each period.

There's also a playground, bocce courts, roller hockey rink, shuffleboard, ball fields, and picnic areas. The beach is located at Father Capadanno Boulevard and Sand Lane.

**South Beach**
**Phone: 718-816-6804**

January 1910, an assistant keeper named Smith was rowing to Staten Island in the evening when he lost his bearings and became lost in the dark. Smith finally went ashore at Hoffman Island around 5:00 in the morning. A watchman on the island assisted him. Although he had suffered greatly from his exposure to the cold, by that afternoon Smith was back in his boat, rowing for Staten Island.

Keeper Ed Burge brought a fox terrier to the lighthouse in 1901. Burge recalled Buster in an interview. "You couldn't get that dog to live ashore," he said. "Sometimes when I took him with me after supplies, he'd run down to the edge of the water and look out toward the light, and whine. If the light dimmed at night, or the fog signals stopped, he'd bark and tear around."

Burge claimed that the dog recognized many of the passing boats and loved to sleep outside, keeping an eye on the passing traffic. In 1906, when Burge moved on to Elm Tree Light on Staten Island, the dog was so homesick that Burge gave him to the new keeper at West Bank.

A 1915 article reported that when the passenger steamer *Sandy Hook* passed by twice daily, the keeper, Robert Buske, always rowed out to meet the vessel with his dog, Buster, leaping with excitement in the bow. Buster, described as a large, wire-haired Irish terrier, was the successor to the dog Burge had brought to the lighthouse.

When Buske came abeam of the steamer, a crewman tossed down a bundle that included three copies of the *New York Times* for the three keepers at West Bank. The bundle would land in the water, near Buske's boat. Buster delighted in diving into the waves to retrieve the prize. His eagerness was due in part to the invariable tasty treat from the officers' mess that was tucked between the newspapers. Sometimes "a few bonbons" from the passengers were also included.

On one occasion, the bundle was dropped directly into the boat. Buster was so disappointed that Burge appeased him by tossing his cap into the water for the dog to fetch. Buster was a valued member of the lighthouse crew. "He calls me in foggy weather to start the fog signal," said Buske. "He can smoke my pipe and wear my uniform cap, and he don't like the assistants because they don't bring him treats when they go ashore. I always do."

Marvan J. Andrews, the first assistant keeper, was officially commended in the *Lighthouse Service Bulletin* for his actions of September 4, 1930. According to the bulletin, Andrews "rescued two small buoys" from a capsized rowboat. One can safely assume that it was actually two boys, not buoys, that were rescued.

Otto P. Fjelde was the keeper when the Coast Guard took over from the civilian Lighthouse Service in 1939. Fjelde remained a civilian and stayed in charge, working with Coast Guard crews, until 1956.

Life was generally peaceful until late October 1948, when Coast Guardsman Jose Ortiz went downstairs in the tower and discovered his two fellow keepers, Fjelde and William Barton, unconscious. He was unable to revive them, and a fast call to the Coast Guard brought help from Sandy Hook and from Brooklyn.

The two men had to be lowered on stretchers into rubber rafts and then lifted into a plane to be taken to a hospital. The men, who had been overcome by fumes from a coal stove, had improved to fair condition within a few hours.

Charles Kelley of Leonardo, New Jersey, served with Otto Fjelde from 1953 to 1955. "We were on our own then," Kelley said later. "We used our own boat to run for supplies or to go ashore. Rain was once the lighthouse's only source of fresh water, and when storms sent waves splashing over the second-floor catch basins, things got a little salty." Eventually, a tender delivered 2,000 gallons of fresh water every six weeks along with other supplies.

West Bank was the last manned lighthouse in the area when the *New York Times* profiled the crew in 1975.

Five men were assigned to the station, with two or three on duty at a time. Each had two weeks on the station followed by one week ashore. The men on duty served eight-hour watches around the clock.

Food was delivered from Sandy Hook, and the men had a color television (with "incredibly good" reception), a stereo, and a library of paperback books. Civilian visitors weren't allowed into the lighthouse, but in summer it was constantly surrounded by fishermen.

In 1985, West Bank became the last lighthouse in the Third Coast Guard District to be automated. The Fresnel lens was replaced by a modern optic and the Coast Guard crew was reassigned. The light was converted to solar power in 1998.

The Coast Guard declared the lighthouse surplus property in 2007, and it was offered to a suitable new steward under the provisions of the National Historic Lighthouse Preservation Act of 2000. There were no applicants, so it was offered to the general public via an online auction. The high bidder paid $245,000. Although the lighthouse is now privately owned, the Coast Guard will continue to care for the active light and foghorn.

West Bank Light may be seen very distantly from the boardwalk at Coney Island and from South Beach on Staten Island. You may arrange a cruise with Ray Mellett of Sewaren, New Jersey, for an excellent close view; call 973-953-7781.

**West Bank Light in 2008**

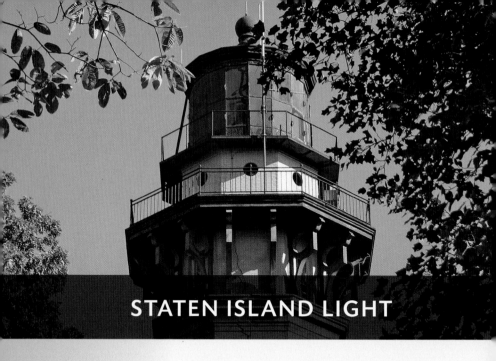

# STATEN ISLAND LIGHT

**Accessibility:** 🔒 🏛

**Geographic coordinates:**
40° 34' 34" N   74° 08' 28" W

**Nearest community:**
Borough of Staten Island,
New York. Located
on Edinboro Road on
Lighthouse Hill.

**Established:** 1912. Present
lighthouse built: 1912.

**Height of tower:**
90 feet. Height of focal
plane: 231 feet.

**Optic:** Second-order Fresnel
lens (1912).

**Characteristic:** Fixed white.

This handsome brick tower stands about two miles from the water in the middle of an upscale neighborhood formerly known as Richmond Hill and now appropriately known as Lighthouse Hill. The neighborhood's opulent homes include the Crimson Beech, the only Frank Lloyd Wright–designed home in New York City.

Congress appropriated $50,000 in June 1906 for the building of a lighthouse on Staten Island to form a range with West Bank Light, which was to be raised in height. The two lights in tandem would help guide mariners through the Ambrose Channel to New York Harbor. A 1908 article in the *New York Times* anticipated the new lighthouse:

> *In conjunction with the Ambrose Channel, what is expected to be the best-equipped lighthouse in the world is to be erected . . . at Richmond, S. I. . . . To Gen. Porter, head of the Lighthouse Board, is due the thanks of the Staten Islanders for the interest which he has shown in obtaining a structure of the highest class of architecture instead of the ordinary lighthouse which is so familiar. The high ground boulevard . . . promises to become a mecca for tourists wishing to enjoy the unusual panoramic view it affords, and to visit the lighthouse, which will be one of the leading objects of interest in New York.*

**Fascinating Fact**

This lighthouse went into service on the same day that the *Titanic* sank, on April 15, 1912.

The Lighthouse Board had requested $100,000 for the project. The West Bank tower was raised in 1908, but because the funding wasn't sufficient, the building of the new lighthouse on Staten Island had to wait for a second appropriation of $50,000 in March 1909.

The lighthouse went into service at sunset on April 15, 1912, less than twenty-four hours after the sinking of the *Titanic*. Had the *Titanic* completed its maiden voyage, it would have made use of the new light as a guide to New York Harbor.

The ninety-foot-tall octagonal tower stands on a limestone base and is built of buff-colored glazed bricks; it's one of the last brick lighthouses constructed in the United States. A state-of-the-art pumping system was installed to send kerosene directly to the lamp. A second-order Fresnel range lens produced a fixed white light, visible only in the channel, two hundred thirty-one feet above the water. Red brick lines the tower, and a 104-step spiral stairway leads to the watch room.

A comfortable two-and-one-half-story keeper's house was built a short distance to the east, also constructed of buff-colored brick with a red roof. The station was originally home to two keepers and their families.

Another *Times* article sang the praises of the new tower: "On Richmond Heights, S. I., there will blaze to-night for the first time a great light that can be seen thirty-five miles at sea." The article compared the Staten Island Light to the world's great lighthouses, including England's Eddystone.

Arthur Anderson, who grew up in the neighborhood and often visited the lighthouse, wrote about a particular visit in the 1920s with a friend in a memoir called *A Richmondtown Childhood*. By this time, the light had been converted to electric operation:

> *Johnny and I noticed a manhole in the lawn a few feet from the lighthouse. We were able to open the cover and found beneath it a concrete*

## SIDE TRIP:
### LaTourette Park

LaTourette Park, which borders on Lighthouse Hill, is a section of Staten Island's Greenbelt and one of the borough's flagship parks. The Greenbelt, at 2,800 acres, is the nation's largest park under municipal jurisdiction.

The 511-acre LaTourette Park encompasses a wide variety of forest habitats and has four main hiking trails. The LaTourette family established a farm on the land in 1830, and the family's 1870 mansion is now the clubhouse for the park's golf course. When there's snow, there's also great sledding in the park. Entrance to LaTourette Park is on Richmond Hill Road.

**LaTourette Park**
**Phone: (212) NEW-YORK**
**For golfing information,**
**call (718) 351-1889.**
**Web site: www.nycgovparks.org/parks/R013/**

*underground chamber. We got flash-lights, climbed down an iron ladder inside, and found that the chamber contained nothing but a large tank that had formerly held the light's kerosene fuel supply. The tank was, of course, empty, but we found a three-foot-long metal bar that must have had some connection with its operation. More than once, we went down into the chamber, banged the bar on the empty tank, and yelled at the top of our lungs. The horrific, ugly sound echoing off the concrete walls was somehow wonderfully satisfying.*

**Staten Island Light in 2008**

The original lens remains in use today, and the automated white light is on day and night. The keeper's house is now privately owned. The tower's attractive architecture earned it a place on the New York City Historical Landmarks list in 1968.

Joseph N. Esposito of Staten Island served as the volunteer caretaker of the light for nine years. Esposito was a master electrician, carpenter, and mason by trade. In 1992, after major Coast Guard budget cuts, he asked about the possibility of becoming the caretaker of the lighthouse. Esposito submitted his résumé and soon had the keys to the tower. "He's been wonderful," Rear Admiral Bennis told the *New York Times*. "We were lean and mean, and we needed someone to take care of the place."

During his years as caretaker, Esposito did everything from cutting the small patch of grass around the tower to explaining the station's history to visitors, as well as making sure the light was operating twenty-four hours a day. On the rare occasions that the light went out, residents of Lighthouse Hill would quickly let Esposito know, and he would fix whatever needed fixing.

When he stepped down for medical reasons, Esposito told the *Times*, "I'm gonna miss her [the lighthouse]. She's the only one like it in the world. Every time I stepped in it, I was going back in time to 1912."

For many years, Esposito also constructed some of the most detailed lighthouse replicas in existence. He said he made the models so he could "see the light when I can't really be there." He was recognized on April 18, 2001, by the Coast Guard in a citation awarded for meritorious service. Reflecting on the end of his lighthouse duties, Esposito said, "I feel like I've lost a dear friend."

The lighthouse stands on Edinboro Road. Because it's necessary to cross private property to reach the grounds immediately around the tower, the grounds are closed to the public. Views of the upper part of the tower are possible on Edinboro and other nearby streets, but houses, trees, and power lines make photographs difficult.

## SIDE TRIP: *Historic Richmond Town*

Not far from Lighthouse Hill on Staten Island is Historic Richmond Town, a living history village and museum complex established in 1958. Here, visitors can explore the history and diversity of Staten Island and its neighboring communities, from the colonial period to the present. The village area is composed of fifteen restored buildings, including homes, commercial buildings, and a museum. Staff and volunteers provide tours and demonstrations on a seasonal basis.

Directions are available on the Historic Richmond Town Web site, or by calling (718) 351-1611.

**Historic Richmond Town**
**441 Clarke Avenue**
**Staten Island, NY 10306**
**Phone: (718) 351-1611**
**Web site: www.historicrichmondtown.org**

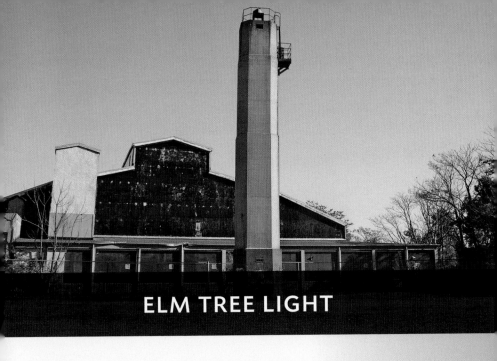

# ELM TREE LIGHT

The abandoned, nondescript concrete tower that now stands near an old airplane hangar at Miller Field on the east coast of Staten Island would never be mistaken for a traditional lighthouse, but for many years an important aid to navigation was located here. Long before that, sailors used a prominent elm tree in the vicinity as a day beacon.

**Accessibility:** 🏠

**Geographic coordinates:** 40° 33' 50" N  74° 05' 43" W

**Nearest community:** Borough of Staten Island, New York. Located at Miller Field, east coast of Staten Island.

**Established:** 1856. Present lighthouse built: 1939. Deactivated: 1964.

**Height of tower:** 65 feet.

**Optic:** Third-order Fresnel lens (1856). Sixth-order Fresnel lens (1939).

**The 1856 Elm Tree Light**

Three new sets of range lights were established in 1856 for the Main, Gedney, and Swash Channels to New York Harbor. The Elm Tree Light served as the front range light in the Swash Channel. The New Dorp Light, nearly two miles distant, served as the rear range light.

A 1797 map described the tree: "Large Elm tree Standing by the Shore a Mark for Vessels leaving and going from New York to Amboy, Middletown, and Brunswick." The old tree was claimed by shoreline erosion by the 1850s, but it was memorialized in the name of the lighthouse that followed it.

The lower part of the original hexagonal wooden tower was surrounded by a system of skeletal supports that flared out, making the tower look something like a rocket. A fixed white light was shown by a third-order Fresnel lens, sixty-two feet above mean high water.

The light was first exhibited on November 1, 1856, and the first keeper was William Hooper. After Hooper died in 1859, his wife, Sarah Ann Hooper, served as keeper until 1867.

For some years, the station fought a battle with the encroaching sea. The 1870 annual report of the Lighthouse Board stated that more than fifty feet

## Fascinating Fact

This tower stands on land that was once a farm owned by William Henry Vanderbilt, the wealthy and prominent businessman.

of land in front of the station had been washed away. To protect the site, the board asked for funds to extend an existing jetty. Congress appropriated $1,500 in March 1871 and the work was completed, but the problem wasn't solved. Additional appropriations were needed in the late 1870s to further lengthen and repair the jetty.

A change in the channel necessitated the moving of the tower a short distance to the northeast in 1891, after an appropriation of $3,000. A plank walk connected the dwelling to the tower, and the tower's supporting braces were lengthened along with other improvements.

Jacob C. Swain was the keeper from 1885 to 1906. Robert Bachand, in his book *Northeast Lights*, informs us that Swain, when he was in his late sixties, married a widow with two children. The couple had two more children, and Sarah Swain assisted her husband with his lightkeeping duties. Swain died in February 1906, leaving Sarah with four children, aged three to fourteen.

## SIDE TRIP: *Miller Field*

Miller Field, a U.S. Air Force facility, was established around the Elm Tree Light Station in 1919–21, on land that was once a farm owned by the Vanderbilt family. It was named for James Ely Miller, the first American aviator killed in World War I. At the time, it was the only coastal air defense station in the country. In 1973, Miller Field was acquired by the National Park Service and became part of the Gateway National Recreation Area. Its 187 acres are filled with athletic fields, playgrounds, and a picnic area.

A 1920 double seaplane hangar is the most important remaining building because of its association with early aviation history. Exhibits on the history of Miller Field are on display at the ranger station in Building 26. The station is open Wednesday through Sunday, 8:30 a.m. to 5:00 p.m.

**Miller Field**
**Gateway National Recreation Area**
**Public Affairs Office**
**210 New York Avenue**
**Staten Island, NY 10305**
**Phone (718) 351-6970**
**Web site: www.nps.gov/gate/** *and*
**www.nyharborparks.org/visit/mifi.**
**html**

Sarah Swain applied for the keeper's position, but she was turned down in favor of Edward Burge, who had been keeper at West Bank Light for several years. The president of Staten Island's Borough of Richmond defended the widow, to no avail.

Burge remained keeper for about thirteen years. In a 1924 interview, he showed himself to be quite a philosopher. "I'm not sure what the fascination of lighthouse keeping is," he said. "Maybe it is the freedom. . . . It may be the love of the sea. You know the sea fascinates a man, some men more than others. You are a little in awe of it always, and sometimes afraid of it, but you never can get away from it. After a man has been in the service for a time, nothing else ever satisfies. Those who quit usually drift back into it."

For some years, the Elm Tree and New Dorp lights were looked after by a single keeper who also cared for Staten Island Light on Lighthouse Hill. John Carlsson retired in 1934 after a thirty-seven-year lighthouse career that included seventeen years

of keeping the three lights. On the occasion of Carlsson's retirement, a *New York Times* writer asked his wife, Anna, if she expected their life to change. She answered in the negative, adding, "He never went anywhere anyway."

In 1939, the extant sixty-five-foot-tall concrete tower replaced the original wooden tower. The tower displayed two lights: an alternating white and green light as a guide to aircraft, and a white light for the Swash Channel Range. The tower was maintained by the City of New York until the range was discontinued in 1964.

The distinctly unphotogenic Elm Tree Light is easily reached by car. From Hylan Boulevard on Staten Island, follow New Dorp Lane along the south side of Miller Field and continue to the end. You'll see the concrete tower standing near an old hangar. On a clear day, if you walk to the edge of the water, you can spot the Romer Shoal and West Bank lighthouses off in the distance.

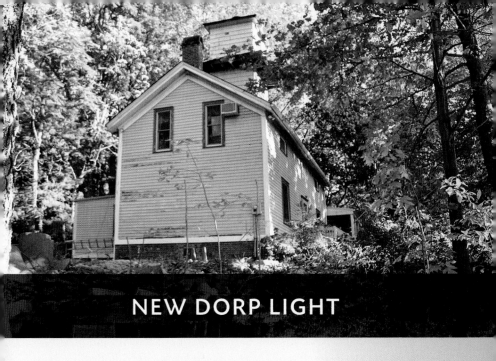

# NEW DORP LIGHT

This light was established in 1856 in the New Dorp (from the Dutch for "new village") section of Staten Island. It served as a rear range light for the Swash Channel, while Elm Tree Light served as the front range light. It was part of a system of three new sets of range lights established after a congressional appropriation of $30,000 in 1852.

**Accessibility:** 🏠 📷

**Geographic coordinates:**
40° 34' 51" N   74° 07' 13" W

**Nearest community:** Borough of Staten Island, New York. Located on a hill in the New Dorp section of Staten Island.

**Established:** 1856. Present lighthouse built: 1856. Deactivated: 1964.

**Height of focal plane:** 192 feet.

**Optic:** Second-order Fresnel lens (1856). Sixth-order Fresnel lens (1939).

The light was displayed from a square wooden tower mounted on the roof of a six-room keeper's dwelling, with a second-order Fresnel range lens showing a fixed red light 192 feet above mean high water. The light was later changed to fixed white.

The style of the building was very similar to the rear lights in the Chapel Hill and Point Comfort ranges. Along with the Elm Tree Light, the light went into service on November 1, 1856. The first keeper was John B. Fountain.

The official right-of-way to the station was a barely passable path up a steep hill on the edge of the Moravian Cemetery, east of the station. For years, the keeper was allowed to use a winding road through the cemetery as

**Late 1800s view**

a much more convenient route. Then, in 1878, the trustees of the cemetery announced that the keeper could no longer use the road.

For more than a decade, Keeper John Langston had to use the difficult path on foot or horseback. Finally, the government gave up its right-of-way path to the cemetery in exchange for the use of the cemetery road.

At some point, a hole was cut in the western side of the lantern. This was probably during the period when a single keeper looked after the New Dorp and Elm Tree lights along with Staten Island Light; from the hole, the keeper could see if the Staten Island Light was lit.

It appears that the family station, located almost two miles from the shore, was quiet and peaceful for most of its history. The Swash Channel range was discontinued in 1964, and the building was boarded up and abandoned.

In 1967, the lighthouse was named a New York City landmark as a "unique vernacular building and unusual design and outstanding architectural character." In spite of this honor, it soon fell victim to the elements and vandals, who stole the copper flashing from its roof and stripped the interior of everything removable.

The federal government auctioned the property in 1975, and the high bidder at $32,000 was a thirty-two-year-old Staten Island engineer named John Vokral. Vokral soon received permission from the New York City Landmarks Preservation Commission to restore the deteriorated building as a home for himself.

"I had been looking for an old house to renovate for a long time because I enjoy doing that type of work," Vokral told the *New York Times*. Over the next couple of years, Vokral "sanded and painted every square inch of that clapboard and hammered every peg into the old floors upstairs—all 1,286 of them."

The only original component Vokral could salvage in the interior was a brass doorknob, and even that was so beaten up it couldn't be used.

## Fascinating Fact

This lighthouse was saved from ruin by its current owner, John Vokral.

Vokral replaced every wall in the building with sheet rock and insulation, and he sanded the exposed beams down to the original wood. The end product, after years of work, was a comfortable and historic home.

The lighthouse remains private property and is off limits to the public, but it is possible to see it from outside the property. From Hylan Boulevard on Staten Island, turn west on New Dorp Lane. Turn right onto Richmond Road, and then turn left onto Altamount Street. Turn left on Beacon Avenue. Take the first right onto Boyle Street. Uphill, off the end of Boyle Street on the right, is the lighthouse.

If you visit, please be sure to respect the privacy of the residents; do not enter the property. Because of the surrounding trees, winter is the best time to get a good view.

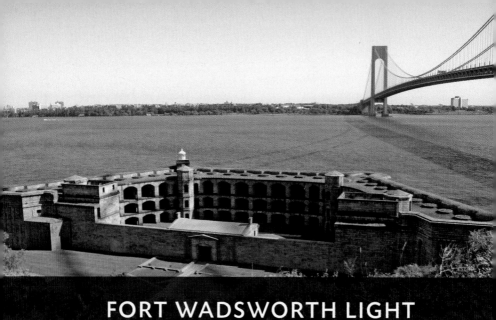

# FORT WADSWORTH LIGHT

**Accessibility:** ♿

**Geographic coordinates:**
40° 36' 21" N   74° 03' 14" W

**Nearest community:**
Borough of Staten Island,
New York. Located on the
northeast corner of Battery
Weed, Fort Wadsworth.

**Established:** 1828 (as
Fort Tompkins Light).
Present lighthouse built:
1903. Deactivated: 1965.
Relighted: 2005

**Height of focal plane:**
75 feet.

**Optic:** Fourth-order Fresnel
lens (1903). Solar powered
modern optic (2005).

The easternmost part of Staten Island, in a strategic position overlooking the Verrazano Narrows leading to New York Harbor, was first fortified by the Dutch with the construction of a blockhouse in 1663. A Patriot redoubt on the site was captured by the British in 1776 and evacuated in 1783.

Early 1900s view of the fort and lighthouse

Construction of a masonry fort on the site began in 1807. The fort was named for Daniel D. Tompkins (1774–1825), governor of New York and the sixth vice president of the United States. The fort was rebuilt in 1847 as a five-sided granite fort with two tiers of casemates and cannons mounted on the third level.

A lighthouse was established at Fort Tompkins in 1828, with a forty-foot-tall tower equipped with a dozen lamps and reflectors. An 1843 inspection report stated that the lighting apparatus was "much worn," and the lantern glass was of poor quality that "would impair and destroy the most brilliant light."

By the time of an 1850 inspection, when John Jennings was keeper, new lighting apparatus had been installed. The new apparatus consisted of nine lamps with twenty-two-inch reflectors. There were still problems; the window frames were decayed and the buildings were in need of whitewashing. In his defense, Jennings had gotten only one night

**Fascinating Fact**

A dedicated band of preservationists restored this lighthouse, leading to its relighting in 2005 after forty years in darkness.

of instruction from his predecessor, Jacob B. Earle.

A fourth-order Fresnel lens replaced the multiple lamps and reflectors in 1855. In the 1860s, the lighthouse's lantern glass suffered damage from artillery practice close by.

A new lighthouse was built in 1873, farther from the fort's cannons. The 1873 structure was an attractive one-and-one-half-story dwelling with gingerbread trim, with a square light tower rising from the front side of its mansard roof.

The name "Fort Wadsworth" was adopted for the military facility in 1864, with several smaller units including Fort Tompkins and Battery Weed. It was named for Brigadier

General James Wadsworth, who died in the Battle of the Wilderness during the Civil War.

Three-tiered Battery Weed, originally called Fort Richmond and built between 1845 and 1861, was renamed in 1863 for Stephen Hinsdale Weed, who was killed defending Little Round Top during the Battle of Gettysburg in the Civil War.

In 1892, the Lighthouse Board stated in its annual report that the light was well back of the point it was intended to mark. The board proposed relocating the light to a corner

**The 1873 Fort Tompkins Lighthouse**

of Battery Weed, along with the addition of a fog bell. At a cost of $696.34, a fog bell with striking machinery was established on the easterly angle of the fort wall on May 16, 1898, with William Boyle designated as its keeper.

In 1900, the Lighthouse Board announced that $12,900 was needed for the relocation of the light. Congress complied with an appropriation in that amount on March 3, 1901, and plans progressed.

In October 1902, while the 1873 lighthouse was still in service, the sad news of a suicide at the lighthouse was reported in newspapers. Alfred L. Carlow, a former keeper of Old Orchard Shoal Light, had been visiting his daughter, who was married to the keeper of Fort Tompkins Light. Carlow hanged himself upstairs in the dwelling. According to a newspaper account, Carlow "had been mentally ill for some time."

A small brick tower was completed, and the light went into operation on May 11, 1903, at the northeast corner of Battery Weed. A fourth-order Fresnel lens displayed a flashing light, alternating red and white, seventy-five feet above mean high water. The fog bell was relocated to the light station, and the keeper's quarters, a small brick building, was moved and remodeled. The 1873 Fort Tompkins Lighthouse has been destroyed in the intervening years.

In the late morning of May 27, 1909, the German steamship *Prinzess Alice* went aground below the lighthouse in thick fog. The station's fog bell was sounding when the accident occurred.

Keeper Nelson Ackerman went outside a few minutes later, as the fog cleared, and was shocked to discover the bow of the ship practically reaching his front door. Ackerman shouted to a crewman, "Hello, when did you get here?" The man replied, "Just arrived." Nobody was injured in the accident, and the steamship was eventually refloated.

In 1941, the light's characteristic was changed from an alternating red and white flash to a green and white

flash. The green flash was intended as an aid for aviators.

The light was automated by the late 1950s, but the station was still maintained by two Coast Guard keepers. The two men in charge in November

## SIDE TRIP:
## Fort Wadsworth

The last military occupant of Fort Wadsworth, the U.S. Navy, left in 1995, and the property was transferred to the Department of the Interior. The fort was opened to the public in 1997 as part of the Gateway National Recreation Area.

Visitors can take a ranger-led tour of the site's many fortifications and get a glimpse of what life was like for soldiers stationed at the Narrows. Tours leave from the visitor center Wednesday through Sunday at 10:00 a.m. and 2:00 p.m. The visitor center is open all year, Wednesday through Sunday, 10:00 a.m. to 4:30 p.m. Interactive exhibits tell the stories of nearly 350 years of fortifications at this site.

**Fort Wadsworth**
**Gateway National Recreation Area**
**Phone: (718) 354-4500**
**Web site: www.nps.gov/gate/ *and***
**www.nyharborparks.org/visit/**
**fowa.html**

1958 were Boatswain Mate First Class Jacob A. Hughes and Engineman First Class Thomas E. Somogyi. The two men lived in a nearby house, Hughes with his wife, Marian, and Somogyi with his wife, Bridget, a daughter, and two stepsons.

Fog had shrouded the fort on November 19 when tensions that had probably been growing for some time boiled over. The two men got into an argument, reportedly over Hughes's wife. According to another report, the fight was the result of growing friction in the tight living quarters.

Somogyi rushed into another room and returned brandishing a claw hammer. Hughes grabbed a kitchen knife, and the two men wrestled. Somogyi fell after being mortally wounded by a knife thrust to the chest.

Hughes phoned for an ambulance and then called the police. He was soon locked in the Army stockade at Governors Island. The twenty-eight-year-old Somogyi, a native of Pennsylvania, was an eight-year veteran of the Coast Guard.

The Verrazano-Narrows Bridge, the world's longest suspension span at the time of its completion, opened in 1964. The bridge joins Staten Island and Brooklyn, connecting to the Staten Island Expressway near Fort Wadsworth. The lighthouse, rendered superfluous by the bridge and its bright lights, was

Fort Wadsworth Light in 2008

discontinued in 1965. Along with the rest of Fort Wadsworth, ownership of the lighthouse passed to the National Park Service in 1995.

The abandoned lighthouse fell into severe disrepair over the years. In 2002, Staten Island resident Joe Esposito, who was also the caretaker of the Staten Island Lighthouse, proposed a restoration plan to Steve Salgo, a Fort Wadsworth park ranger.

Esposito's plan was approved, and soon a band of dedicated volunteers was hard at work on the lighthouse with the goal of restoring it for its one hundredth anniversary in 2003. Thanks largely to the donation of $27,000 in materials by the National Park Service, much restoration was completed within a year.

Esposito and the other volunteers gathered in dense fog on May 10, 2003, to celebrate the anniversary and the restoration. The celebration included a barbecue, a birthday cake, and a special display by two New York City fireboats.

The lighthouse's comeback was capped on September 24, 2005, when it was relit as an aid to navigation. Sadly, Esposito had died six months earlier at the age of sixty-six. His widow, Anna Esposito, flipped the switch at the relighting ceremony, and she was presented with a plaque of appreciation from the National Park Service.

The lighthouse and the grounds around it are not generally open to the public. The best view of the lighthouse is from the park's scenic overlook. The fort is at the east end of Bay Street on Staten Island. To reach Fort Wadsworth from Brooklyn, take the Verrazano-Narrows Bridge to Staten Island and bear right (Bay Street exit) after the tollbooth, then follow the signs to the fort.

From the west, take the Goethals or Bayonne Bridges from New Jersey to the Staten Island Expressway (I-278). Follow the Staten Island Expressway (I-278) east to the Bay Street exit. Turn left at the light and follow this road to Bay Street and the park entrance.

# KINGSBOROUGH COMMUNITY COLLEGE LIGHT

**Accessibility:** 🛗🚗

**Geographic coordinates:** 40° 34' 48" N  73° 56' 00" W

**Nearest community:** Borough of Brooklyn, New York. Located on the campus of Kingsborough Community College, in Brooklyn's Manhattan Beach section.

**Established:** 1990. Present lighthouse built: 1990.

**Height of focal plane:** 114.5 feet.

**Characteristic:** One-second white flash every four seconds.

The skeletal light tower on top of Kingsborough Community College's Marine and Academic Center is one of the newest aids to navigation in the New York Harbor region. Established on December 1, 1990, it shows a one-second white flash every four seconds.

The light tower was part of the original design for the building. Because the seventy-acre campus borders the Sheepshead Bay Channel and Jamaica Bay, the Coast Guard informed college officials that, if they wanted to keep the light, they would have to apply to make it a private aid to navigation. After a formal application, the light received that designation. It's now number 31687 on the official Coast Guard Light List.

Kingsborough Community College, located in the Manhattan Beach section of Brooklyn, was founded in 1963. The site was a training ground for merchant marines during World War II. The Sheepshead Bay facility was the nation's largest training site for the U.S. Maritime Service.

The college serves about thirty thousand students each year and also hosts many community events, including a free summer music festival. The college is an important entry point for Brooklyn residents who choose to pursue higher education. Appropriately, considering its location, the college offers a marine technology curriculum along with many other courses.

The light is best photographed from across Sheepshead Bay in Brooklyn. From the Belt Parkway in Brooklyn, take the Knapp Street/Emmons Avenue exit. At the traffic light, turn left onto Knapp Street, and then turn right onto Emmons Avenue. After a short distance, you'll see the Kingsborough Community College's Marine and Academic Center across the water on your left. There's parking along the street, but spaces can sometimes be hard to come by.

## Fascinating Fact

The site where this building now stands was a training site for merchant marines during World War II.

# CONEY ISLAND LIGHT

**Accessibility:** 🔒

**Geographic coordinates:**
40° 34' 36" N  74° 00' 42" W

**Nearest community:**
Borough of Brooklyn, New York. Located at Norton's Point, the western tip of Coney Island.

**Established:** 1890. Present lighthouse built: 1890. Automated: 1989.

**Height of focal plane:**
75 feet.

**Optic:** Fourth-order Fresnel lens (1890). Vega VRB-25 now in use.

**Characteristic:** Red flash every five seconds.

*C*oney Island, now a peninsula attached to the mainland, was formerly the westernmost of the barrier islands off New York's Long Island. The island was named for its once teeming rabbit population; *coney* is an old word for rabbit.

**Coney Island Light in the 1940s**

A bill "to establish lights at the western end of Coney Island," known as Norton's Point (after a nineteenth-century politician who once ran a hotel at the point), was introduced in Congress in 1888. J. O. Coleman, New York City's commissioner of street cleaning, urged passage of the bill in a February 1889 letter to New York's representatives in Congress. Many vessels, wrote Coleman, including passenger steamers and the tugboats of his own department, had to navigate the narrow channel around Coney Island day and night.

"Life and property are in danger during the continuance of the present condition of things," wrote Coleman, "and it is most urgent that proper safeguards be established at once."

Congress concurred, and $25,000 was appropriated for a light and fog signal in March 1889. The project was delayed when the owners of the property asked for $6,500 for their land, which the government deemed an exorbitant price. The government had the land condemned, and they

**SIDE TRIP: *Coney Island Museum***

Dedicated to the preservation and interpretation of Coney Island history, this museum is full of antiques and relics of the golden years of the Coney Island amusement area. You can also catch a lecture or film here in summer.

The museum is open on Saturdays and Sundays year round from noon to 5:00 p.m. Visiting hours may be expanded during the summer season.

**Coney Island Museum**
**1208 Surf Ave., Brooklyn NY 11224-2816**
**Phone: 718-372-5159**
**Web site: www.coneyisland.com/museum.shtml**

then purchased it for $3,500.

A sixty-eight-foot-tall, square cast-iron skeletal tower with a central cylinder containing a spiral stairway was completed along with a keeper's house in 1890. A similar tower was built in the same year at Throgs Neck at the eastern end of the East River, but that tower no longer stands. The tower type is much more common in the Mid-Atlantic and South; the only similar extant lighthouse in the Northeast is at Marblehead, Massachusetts.

The design of the two-story keeper's house is much like the ones at Gould Island and Castle Hill light stations in Rhode Island, which were established around the same time.

The light went into operation on August 1, 1890, with a fourth-order Fresnel lens showing a flashing red light seventy-five feet above the water. The light served as a guide for mariners passing through the Narrows to New York Harbor. It also served to mark the entrance to Gravesend Bay to the immediate north, and to guide garbage scows to their dumping grounds off-shore. The station's first keeper was Thomas Higgenbotham, a native of Maryland.

Adrien Boisvert was the Coast Guard keeper 1944-60.

The station was established to serve as the rear light in a range, but the front light remained in operation for only six years. The Lighthouse Board announced in 1896 that the site where the front beacon stood would be sold at public auction.

Life for the keepers and their families was mostly quiet just a few miles from the bright lights and crowds of the Coney Island amusement park, which had its heyday in the early 1900s. When the light station was established, the buildings stood alone, with no neighbors in sight. Beginning in the late 1800s, a private community called Sea Gate took shape around the station. The government eventually had to pay $5,000 for a right-of-way through the community.

Among Sea Gate's residents was the future Nobel Prize–winning author Isaac Bashevis Singer, who rented a room near the light station in the winter of 1935 for four dollars a week. "At night the wind howled,"

## SIDE TRIP: *Coney Island Amusement Area*

The remaining attractions at Coney Island are only a shadow of what was there a century ago, but there's still plenty of family fun to be had. The current rides and attractions are generally open from Memorial Day to Labor Day, and weekends only from Easter to Memorial Day and from Labor Day to the end of September.

Among the major attractions are the Astroland Amusement Park, home of the world-famous Cyclone roller coaster, and Deno's Wonder Wheel, with its 150-foot-high Ferris wheel. Nathan's Famous Hot Dogs has been here for more than ninety years and is the home of the Nathan's Famous Fourth of July International Hot Dog Eating Contest, held each year since 1916. In the summer season, you can enjoy fireworks on the beach every Friday night.

To reach Coney Island, take the Belt Parkway to exit 6. Head south on Cropsey Avenue to West 17th Street. Keyspan Park and the Parachute Jump will be in front of you on Surf Avenue. Parking is available along most streets. There are commercial parking lots on West 17th Street and West 12th Street between Mermaid and Surf, West 15th Street between the Boardwalk and Surf, and on Neptune Avenue between West 12th and Stillwell Avenue.

By public transportation, take the D, Q, N, or F train to Stillwell Avenue (last stop). This takes about 45 minutes from midtown Manhattan.

**For more information on Coney Island, visit www.coneyisland.com on the Web.**

---

wrote Singer, "the bell of the lighthouse rang, the ocean stormed and foamed with a rage as old as eternity." Other Sea Gate residents have included songwriter Woody Guthrie and opera singer Beverly Sills.

Erosion took its toll at the light station, and a 600-foot stone wall was built in 1915 for protection. Just a few months later, a storm undermined the wall. It was repaired, but in April 1918, the station's fog bell fell over the eroding bank. A new skeletal bell tower was erected with a 1,200-pound bell, and more riprap stone was added around the station to guard against further encroachment by the sea.

Adrien J. Boisvert, the keeper for the Coast Guard from 1944 to 1960, lived at the station with his wife, Alice, and their seven children. His daughter, Cecile Boisvert Chenette, shared her memories of the station in a 2001 article in *Lighthouse Digest*.

Cecile Boisvert Chenette recalled watching Coney Island fireworks from the lighthouse with her siblings, with a large bag of popcorn prepared by her mother. "We would go up the lighthouse stairs to the outside balcony on the top and sit there with our legs dangling over the railing and have the best time watching the fireworks," she wrote.

Cecile and the other children also helped with some of the lighthouse chores:

*One of our jobs on the Coney Island station was to climb the stairs to the lighthouse each night before sunset. At the top of the lighthouse was a large brass crank*

*handle attached to a cable that held a round weighted barrel. Every night we took turns cranking up the weight. During the night the weight would slowly descend and turn the lens, sending out a beacon of red flashing light. My parents gave me five cents for the job.*

Cecile recalled seeing the ocean liner *Stockholm* pass the station after its collision with the *Andrea Doria* in July 1956. When they saw the front of the ship crumpled like aluminum foil, the family wondered how the ship stayed afloat. The *Ile de France*, carrying survivors from the *Andrea Doria*, passed by later. "We could hear the music softly playing across the still shimmering water, and we could see the survivors on the deck," Cecile wrote. "These people were so lucky to be saved, unlike the forty-six who lost their lives. The music from the ship, the beautiful lights, and the cool summer breeze made it a night to remember."

Cecile's sister, Celestine (Sally) Boisvert O'Connor, recalled the station's fog bell:

## Fascinating Fact

Frank Schubert, the last keeper in the country from the old Lighthouse Service, lived at this light station from 1960 to 2003.

*One of the duties my parents had was to watch out for fog so that they could turn on the fog bell. They were often awakened at night with the sound of distant ships' horns. I remember Dad putting a ladder up on the bell tower during a power outage in order to manually sound the bell with a hammer. He and my brother Adrien Jr. (Andy) would take turns doing this until the fog was gone. Eventually the bell was removed due to shorefront erosion and the fact that modern ships have new ways of establishing their location.*

Coney Island's last lighthouse keeper, Frank Schubert, was born on September 13, 1915, on Staten Island, as the middle of seven children. His father was a carpenter, and young Frank learned all kinds of do-it-yourself skills as a boy. After high school, he got a job through the Works Progress Administration as a lifeguard and swimming instructor at a public pool. He showed an affinity for the water and exhibited strong lifesaving skills.

In 1937, Schubert joined the civilian Lighthouse Service as a seaman on the tender *Tulip*. When the Coast Guard took over the nation's lighthouses in 1939, it was decided that civilians would no longer serve on tenders and lightships.

Rather than join the Coast Guard, Schubert took a position as keeper of Old Orchard Shoal Light, an offshore light near Staten Island. After about three years at Old Orchard Shoal, Schubert was transferred to

**Keeper Frank Schubert playing golf with his grandsons**

New York's Governors Island, where he tended several small aids to navigation around the island.

When the Coast Guard took over the operation of lighthouses, Lighthouse Service keepers were given the option of remaining civilians or joining the Coast Guard. Schubert chose to remain a civilian. As it turned out, he entered another branch of the military in 1942 when he was drafted to serve in World War II.

Schubert told the authorities he was tired of being on and around boats, so he chose to go into the army instead of the navy. The strategy backfired when he was sent to Florida's Camp Gordon to work as a landing craft instructor. Later, he captained combat and utility boats in Japan and the Philippines.

Following his military service, Schubert returned to Governors Island and remained there for another sixteen years. He was then transferred to the lighthouse that would be his home for the rest of his life. Schubert, his wife Marie, and their three children, Francine, Thomas, and Kenneth, moved into the keeper's cottage at Coney Island Light Station in July 1960.

Schubert witnessed many changes and some unusual events in his decades at Coney Island. He once found an eighteen-foot whale stranded near the lighthouse. He saw boats run aground nearby, and he was credited with fifteen rescues in the vicinity of the station. In 1973, a cargo ship collided with a tanker offshore, and Schubert acted quickly to summon the help of the Coast Guard and other emergency personnel. Sixteen seamen were lost in the explosion and fire, but sixty-three were rescued.

Schubert also watched the construction of new houses crowding in around his home and was even startled to see nude bathers. Some of his neighbors weren't always happy with the foghorn that sounded every ten seconds, but as the keeper explained, "When there's a fog, it has to be done."

As the years passed, life for the

extended Schubert family often revolved around the light station. Frank's son Kenneth was married there. Despite the closeness of New York City and its many entertainment offerings, Frank was happy staying close to home. In 1986, he told a reporter that he and his wife hadn't seen a movie since 1946, adding, "we haven't taken a vacation in twenty years." Marie corrected him: "Twenty-five."

Coney Island Lighthouse was automated in 1989, but the Coast Guard retained Schubert as the resident caretaker. He told the *New York Times*, "I'm a relic. The Coast Guard wants me to stay on, and I surely don't want to leave. My plan is to stay as long as I live." He continued to maintain the grounds and kept a close eye on the light and fog signal, climbing the eighty-seven steps in the tower daily.

As the years went by and the remaining employees of the Lighthouse Service passed into history, Frank Schubert increasingly got

## SIDE TRIP:
### *New York Aquarium*

New York City's only aquarium features over 8,000 creatures from Africa to the Arctic and also displays local species from the Hudson River. Here you can see California sea lions, walruses, sharks, penguins, sea otters, and much more. Weekend programs feature the performing arts and activities for families.

New York Aquarium, open 365 days a year, is located on Surf Avenue and West 8th Street in the Coney Island section of Brooklyn. For directions, call the aquarium or check online.

**New York Aquarium**
**Phone: (718) 265-FISH**
**Web site: www.nyaquarium.com**

more attention. He visited the White House in 1989 as the guest of President George H. W. Bush. Schubert said the president was "nuts about lighthouses."

Not all the attention was welcomed. After he was interviewed on a public radio program in 2002, Schubert was inundated with visitors. A *Times* article quoted him, "I've gotten discovered and now people won't leave me alone. People think there's something romantic about a lighthouse. It's just a lighthouse. I don't understand it, really."

Reporters pretended to be handymen or relatives to get access. "The guy can't sit and have a cup of coffee without being bothered," said Petty Officer Frank Bari of the Coast Guard. "He doesn't mind talking now and then.

Frank Schubert, the last keeper of the old Lighthouse Service

But how would you feel?" Still, Schubert was cordial and accommodating to countless visitors.

When Schubert's children were young, they had their chores to do at the light station, including the winding of the clockwork mechanism that rotated the lens. His grandson Scott Schubert has said that he and his cousins followed suit, doing chores at the station like mowing the lawn, painting fences, and providing tours to visitors since they were old enough to take the responsibility. "This is our way of giving back for all the memories and fun we've had over the years," said Scott, who now maintains a Web site about the light station and his grandfather.

In 2002, Schubert told a *New York Daily News* reporter that once he moved to the Coney Island Lighthouse he never wanted to live anywhere else. "I love it here," he said. "The privacy, the neighbors. Why would I leave? I love it so much."

Frank Schubert didn't retire, and he didn't leave. He remained at the light he loved until the end of his years. He died at eighty-eight on December 11, 2003, in the seven-room keeper's cottage where he had spent forty-three years as keeper and caretaker. The passing of Frank Schubert, believed to be the last living person who served as a lighthouse keeper under the old Lighthouse Service, truly marked the end of an era.

Master Chief Tony Gray of Coast Guard Aids to Navigation New York said that the Coast Guard considered Schubert a true lighthouse keeper until the end of his life. "He'd call us if there were any problems," said Gray, "not only with the lighthouse but with the other aids in the area." Master Chief Gray said he spoke with Schubert three days before his death and that he "seemed like a fifty-five-year-old man. He was a really nice guy."

The lighthouse stands off Surf Avenue, between B47 and B48 streets in the gated community of Sea Gate. You can drive to the gate and explain that you'd like to photograph the lighthouse, but lighthouse hunters will not

**Coney Island Light in 2008**

necessarily be granted entrance. You may photograph the lighthouse from the water; one possibility is to charter a cruise with Ray Mellett of Sewaren, New Jersey (973-953-7781).

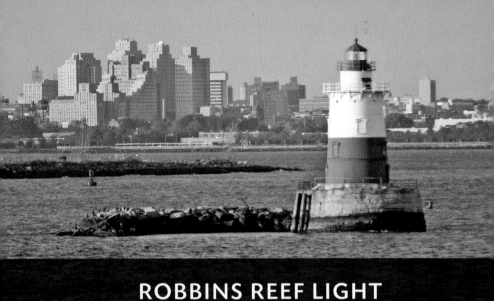

# ROBBINS REEF LIGHT

**Accessibility:** ⚓

**Geographic coordinates:**
40° 39' 27" N   74° 03' 55" W

**Nearest community:**
Bayonne, New Jersey.
Located on the west side of
Upper New York Bay, near
the entrance to the Kill Van
Kull.

**Established:** 1839. Present
lighthouse built: 1883.
Automated: ca. 1964.

**Height of tower:** 45 feet.
Height of focal plane: 56
feet.

**Optic:** Fixed fourth-order
Fresnel lens (1855). Rotating
fourth-order Fresnel lens
(1883). Now 300 mm optic.

**Characteristic:** Green flash
every six seconds.

Robbins Reef, an obstruction off the northern tip of Staten Island in Upper New York Bay, was a menace to harbor traffic and also to shipping passing through the Kill Van Kull to Newark Bay. Although it's a familiar New York Harbor landmark and has often been listed as a New York light, the lighthouse is clearly located in New Jersey waters by about a half mile.

The reef takes its name from the harbor seals that were once plentiful in the vicinity; *robyn* is an old Dutch word for seal. In the days of New Amsterdam, Dutch boys rowed to the reef to shoot seals with their blunderbusses.

Late 1800s illustration

Congress appropriated $50,000 for a lighthouse on the reef in March 1837. It was determined that the foundation, forty-eight feet in diameter and eighteen feet in elevation, would be built of granite to protect against floating ice. The contractor, Daniel Haselton, who had been involved in the construction of a similar tower at Whaleback Ledge in Maine several years earlier, built an octagonal granite lighthouse tower atop the foundation.

Accommodations for a keeper and his family were inside the tower. The first keeper, Isaac Johnson, lighted the multiple lamps and reflectors for the first time on October 25, 1839. A fixed white light was displayed, sixty-six feet above the water.

An 1851 inspection report called the lighthouse "well built, dry, and in good preservation," but the fifteen fourteen-inch reflectors were "too small, too many for good economy, and badly placed." The apparatus was soon replaced by nine lamps with twenty-one-inch reflectors.

The 1851 report was also critical of a recent paint job: "Floors of dwelling, steps of tower, and everything that could be painted, was covered. Wasteful expenditure of paint." The keeper, Richard Cary, was absent at the time of the inspection, and the officials found a sixteen-year-old boy in charge.

A fourth-order Fresnel lens

replaced the multiple lamps and reflectors in 1855. The station had a seven-hundred-pound fog bell with striking machinery as early as 1851. A bell remained in service until a fog siren went into operation in April 1893.

The original tower had deteriorated and was in need of replacement by the 1880s. With a lightship temporarily in place near the reef, the old stone tower was torn down and a cast-iron tower was built in its place. The new four-story lighthouse on a round granite foundation went into service on July 10, 1883, with a rotating fourth-order Fresnel lens showing a white flash every six seconds.

Even with the lighthouse and fog signal, occasional accidents occurred on the reef—often attributable to the heavy harbor traffic. In October 1890, the passenger steamer *City of Rome* went aground on the reef with more than six hundred passengers while attempting to avoid a line of canal boats being towed. All the passengers were safely removed to other vessels, and the steamer was refloated at high tide. In December 1923, the gigantic steamship *Leviathan* grounded on the reef at the end of a transatlantic voyage, necessitating extensive repairs.

Kate Walker, who would become one of the most famous lighthouse keepers in the world, was born Katherine Gortler in Germany in 1846. She journeyed to America with a young son after her first husband, Jacob Kaird, died. While working at a boarding house at Sandy Hook, New Jersey, in the early 1880s, she met John Walker, an assistant keeper at the Sandy Hook Light Station. Walker provided free English lessons for Kate, and romance quickly blossomed.

Before long, Kate and John were

## Fascinating Fact

Kate Walker, this lighthouse's longtime keeper, stood less than five feet tall but was credited with saving at least fifty people from drowning.

married. "He took me to that light-house as his bride," Kate said years later. "I enjoyed life there, for the light was on land, and we could have a gar-den and raise flowers." The Walkers once traveled to the Catskills; it would be the last time Kate would travel beyond the New York Harbor area for the rest of her life.

Kate's world changed dramati-cally after her husband was appointed keeper at Robbins Reef. There was no land around the lighthouse, just a small stone pier. Kate later described her reaction when she and John arrived at their new home. "The day we came, I said to him, 'I can't stay here. The sight of water every-where I look makes me too lonesome.' I refused to unpack my trunks, but somehow they got unpacked." Kate became her husband's official assis-tant at $350 per year, and she grad-ually grew accustomed to her new home in the harbor.

In 1886, John Walker caught a severe cold that developed into pneu-monia, and he had to be rowed to

**Keeper Kate Walker on the ladder at Rob-bins Reef**

Staten Island for medical attention. Legend has it that John's last words to Kate were, "Mind the light, Kate." Someone had to stay at the lighthouse, so Kate couldn't accompany her hus-band to the hospital.

Years later, Kate recalled what happened next. "A few nights later as I was sitting here tending the lamp, I saw a boat coming. Something told me the news it was bringing. I expected to hear the voice that came up out of the dark. 'We're sorry, but your husband's worse.' 'You mean he's dead?' I answered, and they made no reply." Kate was widowed for the second time at the age of forty, with two children to care for.

Some doubted that Kate would be physically capable of handling the duties at the lighthouse by herself, but she applied for and received the keeper position. It was a rare case of a woman being appointed keeper of a lighthouse that was surrounded by water. She grew to love her unique life at the station. "You have nature and the elements," she said in 1925, "and the best company of all—the quiet."

Kate Walker stood barely four-foot ten with her shoes on. Like so many celebrated keepers, she downplayed the difficulties and isolation of her unique post. "Oh, there were so many things at the lighthouse," she said in 1925. "It's so funny to hear people call it a lonely place."

When they were young, Kate rowed her children—Jake and Mary—to Staten Island so they could attend school. At night, she had to wind the mechanism that rotated the lighthouse lens every three hours, so she napped during the afternoon.

In winter, it wasn't unusual for Kate to spend the entire night in the lantern, making sure the glass stayed clear of frost. After drinking a cup of coffee delivered by her son at dawn, Kate would go to bed—unless, of course, foggy conditions necessitated the starting of the fog signal.

Kate's children assisted their mother with the light as they got older, but Kate rarely got a good night's

**Keeper Kate Walker inside the lighthouse**

sleep. "Even when I am off duty," she said, "I wake up every hour in the night to see if the light is all right. You get a thing like that on your mind. The light must be kept burning."

It was said that Kate could recognize every ship that frequented the harbor by the sound of its whistle. Once, while in New York City, she heard a steam whistle at a factory that made her stop in her tracks. "If I didn't know that the *Richard B. Morse* had been scrapped years ago," she said, "I would have said that was her whistle." Someone checked into the matter, and sure enough—the factory's whistle had been salvaged from the *Morse*.

By her own account, Kate saved fifty people from drowning during her years at the lighthouse, but estimates by others range as high as seventy-five. One of the most memorable rescues occurred on a winter night when a schooner crashed into the reef. Kate launched her small boat in heavy seas and rescued all five of the crew, bringing them into the lighthouse.

When one of the men asked,

"Where's Scottie?" Kate rushed back outside to rescue a small Scottie dog. She nursed the dog back to health for the next few days. When the captain returned to pick up his beloved pet, the dog looked at Kate. "That's when I learned dogs could weep," she said later. "There were tears in his eyes."

Another of Kate's most dramatic rescues occurred on October 1, 1909, when the motor launch *Clare*, from Bayonne, New Jersey, plowed into the reef with eight men on board. The boat overturned, throwing the passengers into the waves. Kate swiftly launched her rowboat and single handedly pulled two of the men on board, just as they were becoming exhausted from struggling in the water. A party on a nearby powerboat came to the scene, and soon all of the *Clare*'s passengers were saved.

Kate's son, Jake, eventually served as the assistant keeper, and he lived at the lighthouse with his wife and their three young daughters. Jake frequently rowed to shore to get supplies, often in dangerous conditions. Once, on New Year's Day, he tried to row into a cold wind from Staten Island back to the lighthouse with a turkey and fixings intended for New Year's dinner. After three hours of struggling against the elements, he had to turn back. There was no New Year's dinner at the lighthouse that year.

Each Christmas Eve, Jake Walker rowed his wife and three daughters to the St. George section of Staten Island so that they could buy presents for each other. This was one of the few times the little girls saw anyone outside of the family. When a rare visitor came to the lighthouse, the two youngest girls invariably hid behind their grandmother's skirts. When the girls reached school age, they moved to the mainland with their mother, while their father split his time between the mainland home and the lighthouse.

In 1902, a newspaper reporter asked Kate why she had never taken her allotted vacation time. "Ach!" she replied. "I wouldn't know what to do with a whole day on shore—and

then, I love the light." Kate Walker knew no fear at the lighthouse, but visits to the mainland were a different story, "I have only known fear on land," she once said. "I am afraid of streetcars and automobiles. I have to go to New York about twice a year on business. I am in fear from the time I leave the ferryboat."

One of the worst storms Kate Walker experienced was one Christmas night, while the rest of the family was ashore. She described the storm in an interview:

> Above the wind, I heard something that chilled me. I had heard it only twice before in twenty-five years. My one link with the outside world was a rowboat hung on the outer wall by chains. If the chains broke, the boat would be swept away. It was the clanking of the boat chain that I had heard.
>
> I opened the door of the porch, but the wind flung me back. I tried again and again, but it hurled me back and slammed the door. The third time, I fell, and crawled along

*the stone pier to the side where the boat was hung. Every moment I feared I would be swept into the sea by the waves. The wind nearly whirled me off the landing into the sea, and I had to fight for breath. The sleet froze on me. Finally I managed to tie the boat fast so that it could not move.*

The storm continued to batter the lighthouse with wind, waves, and ice for three days before the sun finally appeared. Her family returned to the lighthouse, and Kate's lonely ordeal was over.

Kate remained keeper until 1919. She retired to a small home in Tompkinsville on Staten Island, and she died in February 1931, at the age of eighty-four, after a long illness.

Kate Walker will never be forgotten for the long years she served the mariners of New York Harbor,

honoring her husband's last request. "We buried him on the mainland over there," Kate once said of her husband. "Every morning when the sun comes up, I stand at the porthole and look towards his grave. Sometimes the hills are brown, sometimes they are green, sometimes they are white with snow. But always they bring a message from him—something I

Robbins Reef Light in 2008

heard him say more often than anything else. Just three words— 'Mind the light.'"

During the Coast Guard era, four men were assigned to Robbins Reef. Three men staffed the station at a time, with the fourth on shore for five days' leave. The Coast Guard crew was removed in the mid-1960s, and for some years, the light was controlled from the St. George Coast Guard station.

A 175-foot Coast Guard buoy tender, the *Katherine Walker*, was launched in 1996. One of several "keeper class" tenders named for heroic lighthouse keepers, the *Walker* is home-ported in Bayonne, New Jersey, within sight of Robbins Reef.

Robbins Reef Light may be easily seen from the decks of the Staten Island Ferry (free), although the view is rather distant. For information on the ferry, call 718-876-8441 or visit www.nyc.gov online.

For a closer view, you can charter a cruise with Ray Mellett of Sewaren, New Jersey (973-953-7781). Near the lighthouse is a stone structure that could be easily mistaken for the base of the 1839 lighthouse; it's actually a sewer outfall constructed around 1915.

# TITANIC MEMORIAL LIGHTHOUSE

This tower stands today near the buildings of the South Street Seaport Museum, at the corner of Fuller and Pearl streets at the southern end of Manhattan. From 1913 to 1968, it was a familiar sight to mariners and landlubbers alike in its location atop the Seaman's Church Institute, overlooking the East River at South Street and Coenties Slip.

**Accessibility:** 🚗 🧍

**Geographic coordinates:**
40° 42' 27" N   74° 00' 14" W

**Nearest community:** New York City. Located at the corner of Fuller and Pearl streets at the entrance to the South Street Seaport, in Lower Manhattan.

**Established:** 1913. Present lighthouse built: 1913. Moved to present location: 1976.

**Height of tower:** 60 feet.

The Seaman's Church Institute was founded as a relief society in 1834 and is affiliated with the Episcopal Church. The institute today is the largest mariners' agency in North America; its educational facilities provide navigational training to nearly 1,600 mariners yearly, and its chaplains visit around 3,400 vessels each year, mostly in New York and New Jersey.

The lighthouse as it originally looked

In the early years of the twentieth century, the Seaman's Church Institute announced plans for a new twelve-story headquarters building in Lower Manhattan, a Flemish-style building to be topped by a lighthouse that would welcome incoming seafarers. The building was to include hundreds of rooms that would serve as transient rooms for mariners.

The cornerstone was laid on April 16, 1912, one day after the news of the sinking of the *Titanic* reached New York. The luxury liner was on route to New York City on its maiden voyage, and many prominent New Yorkers were among the fifteen hundred lives lost.

A newspaper noted that the voices of many at the dedication ceremony broke with emotion when they tried to sing, "Oh hear us when we cry to Thee, for those in peril on the sea."

A lighthouse was part of the existing plan for the building, but it was relabeled a memorial after the *Titanic* disaster. There was much arguing among the thirty-two-member Titanic Memorial Committee about the design. One businessman proposed building the largest lighthouse in the world, and a banker suggested a statue depicting the *Titanic* hitting an iceberg. The committee finally agreed

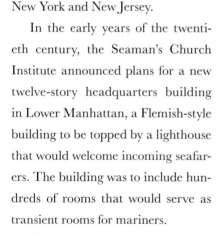

on a relatively modest design.

The round lighthouse had stairs in the rear, and it displayed a fixed green light visible throughout New York Harbor and all the way through the Narrows to Sandy Hook. Surmounting the tower was a time ball, to be hoisted five minutes before noon, Monday through Friday, and dropped at the precise moment a telegraphic signal signifying noon was received from Washington, D.C.

The Titanic Memorial Lighthouse was dedicated on April 16, 1913, in the presence of more than two hundred people, including some relatives and friends of *Titanic* victims.

Bishop David H. Greer of New York spoke at the dedication. "The service that brings us together today," he said, "is of great significance. We commemorate the exhibition of some of the finest and noblest elements of human nature. But this memorial service is something more than that. It is meant to perpetuate not only the human values on that occasion lost, but the human values on that occasion

The Seaman's Church Institute building as it looked with the lighthouse on its roof

**Fascinating Fact**

From 1913 to 1968, this lighthouse stood on the roof of the Seaman's Church Institute headquarters in Lower Manhattan.

found, which were then revealed."

Bishop Greer read the dedication of the lighthouse: "As its light by night shall guide pilgrims and seafaring men from every clime into this port, so may they follow Him who is the Light of Life across the waves of this troublesome world to everlasting life; and, looking at noon toward this place to note the time of day, may they remember that our days pass as the swift ships, and in view of the shortness and uncertainty of human life, strive to fulfill their duty well, as the best preparation for Eternity. Amen."

It became fashionable, according to author Jim Crowley, for passersby to set their watches to the drop of the ball at noon each day. Crowley remembered his father, who worked on the docks in Brooklyn, setting his old Timex to synchronize with the lighthouse.

The daily ball drop continued until the mid-1960s, when the Seaman's Church Institute put the building up for sale. After the organization relocated, the building was demolished.

## SIDE TRIP: *South Street Seaport Museum*

The South Street Seaport Museum was formed in 1967 to save eleven blocks of historic buildings in Lower Manhattan from the wrecker's ball. The museum's founders, with the help of real estate developers, were able to buy most of the buildings. They then established a maritime museum and library designed to tell the story of New York's maritime history and culture.

Within a twelve-square-block radius, the museum now boasts more than 30,000 square feet of exhibit space and educational facilities. It's also home port to an impressive fleet of historic vessels, including the *Peking*, a 1911 bark, the *Wavertree*, an 1885 cargo ship, and the Ambrose Lightship.

In addition to its permanent collection of maritime paintings, ocean liner memorabilia, scrimshaw, ship models, and much more, the museum offers extensive changing exhibits along with a range of family programs. The museum's gift shop at 211 Water Street is also a working letterpress office using nineteenth-century presses.

There are many ways to reach the museum by car or public transportation; contact the museum or check their Web site for details.

**South Street Seaport Museum**
**12 Fulton Street**
**New York City, NY 10038**
**Phone: 212-748-8600.**
**Web site: www.southstreetseaportmuseum.org**

Memorial plaque for the *Titanic* on the lighthouse

The lighthouse was removed in 1968 by the Kaiser-Nelson Steel & Salvage Corporation and donated to the South Street Seaport Museum. In May 1976, it was erected at its present location, with funds provided by the Exxon Corporation. The concrete lower portion of the tower is not original.

This historic structure remains the only significant memorial to the *Titanic* victims as a group. The lighthouse is at the corner of Fuller and Pearl streets at the entrance to the South Street Seaport. It's within walking distance of the Staten Island Ferry's Whitehall Terminal, and it's near the Fulton Street stop on the M15 bus line. By subway, you can take the 2, 3, 4, 5, Z, or M trains to Fulton Street

The Titanic Memorial Lighthouse in 2008

and walk toward the water to Pearl Street. For driving directions, check www.southstreetseaportmuseum.org or call 212-748-8600.

# AMBROSE LIGHTSHIP AND TOWER

**Accessibility:** (Ambrose Lightship at South Street Seaport) 🏢 🚶 🏠

**Geographic coordinates:** (Ambrose Light Tower) 40° 27' 36" N   73° 49' 48" W (The Ambrose Lightship is now located at Pier 16 at the South Street Seaport in New York City.)

**Established:** (lightship) 1908, (tower) 1967. Automated: 1988. Discontinued: (tower) 2008.

A ninety-foot-long wooden-hulled vessel anchored about thirteen miles east/southeast of Sandy Hook in 1823 was the first American lightship in the open ocean. Except for the period of 1829–38, a lightship remained at the station, serving as a floating lighthouse to help guide mariners headed to New York Harbor.

Ambrose Lightship and Ambrose Light Tower in 1967

# BUSINESS REPLY MAIL
FIRST-CLASS MAIL   PERMIT NO. 210   FLAGLER BEACH FL

POSTAGE WILL BE PAID BY ADDRESSEE

**GUNS&AMMO**

PO BOX 421124
PALM COAST FL  32142-9171

A new main channel into the Port of New York, two thousand feet wide and forty-five feet deep, was dredged in the early 1900s after an appropriation of $6 million. The channel was named for John Wolf Ambrose, a New York businessman whose pleas led the federal government to improve the channels to the harbor. Ambrose died at sixty-one in 1899, before the channel named for him was established.

In 1904, the Lighthouse Board recommended a lightship with a fog signal at the eastern entrance to the Ambrose Channel. The Sandy Hook lightship station was relocated slightly to the entrance to the channel and was renamed Ambrose. The last vessel at the Sandy Hook station, the *LV 51*, was reassigned to relief duty.

A new ship, the *LV 87*, was built at Camden, New Jersey, for the Ambrose station at a cost of $99,000. The *LV 87* went into service on December 1, 1908, and it remained at the Ambrose station until 1932. Once the light was established, mariners heading to New York Harbor from the east

## Fascinating Fact

The *LV 87*, the ship that served at this station from 1908 to 1932, is open to the public at the South Street Seaport; it's one of fewer than twenty surviving lightships in the United States.

**Ambrose Light Tower, built in 1967**

would, upon reaching the Nantucket Lightship off Cape Cod, aim for the Ambrose Lightship.

The 112-foot-long, steel-hulled vessel had two masts with three oil lens lanterns on each mast, but it was

quickly converted to electric operation. The steam-powered ship was
originally schooner-rigged in an effort
to reduce rolling in heavy seas, but the
sails and rigging were removed early
in the *LV 87*'s career. In addition to its
lights, the vessel was equipped with a
fog whistle and a submarine bell for
many years.

The captain of the *LV 87* for all of
its years at the Ambrose station was
Gustave A. Lange, a Staten Island
native who had gone to sea at the age
of fourteen and was in command of
a trading vessel by the time he was
nineteen. While he was in charge
of the lightship, Lange's wife and
three children lived in Queens, New
York. A few days of shore leave each
month allowed for brief visits with
his family.

Lange and his crew had some
anxious moments during World War I
when a German submarine was spotted nearby. It was especially discon-
certing because the lightship at Diamond Shoals off Cape Hatteras had
just been sunk, but the submarine

departed without incident.

The *LV 87* parted anchor and
drifted from its station during a February 1927 gale. Lange was able to
steer it to the lighthouse depot on
Staten Island, and it was back on its
location a week later.

In 1929, quick thinking by Lange
averted a near-tragedy. A relief lightship, the *LV 111*, was on the way
to the Ambrose station with Lang
on board. The vessel was passing
the passenger liner *Santa Barbara*,
which signaled him to pass in front
of its bow. The *Santa Barbara* swiftly
approached, and Lange realized that
there wasn't enough time to pass in
front of the huge ship without the
lightship being cut in two. He swung
the lightship around so that the two
vessels struck head on, resulting in
significantly less damage.

The *LV 87* became a relief vessel
in 1932, and the *LV 111* took its place
at the Ambrose station. The *LV 111*,
which was 132 feet long, was the first
American lightship with full diesel
propulsion when it was built in 1926.

Lange remained captain at the station until his retirement in 1936, and the *LV 111* served at the Ambrose channel until 1952, when it was relocated to Portland, Maine. The *LV 111* rode out the calamitous hurricane of September 21, 1938, when winds at the station topped seventy-five miles per hour, with thirty-five to forty-five-foot seas.

A relief lightship on the station in heavy fog on June 24, 1960, was struck by a freighter, the *Green Bay*. The lightship sank to the bottom within ten minutes, but the crew of nine was safely rescued. The vessel still sits on the bottom in about one hundred feet of water.

The last vessel to serve on the Ambrose station was the *WLV 613*, a 128-foot-long diesel-propelled vessel built at Curtis Bay, Maryland, in 1952. The vessel was removed in 1967, when it was replaced by a $2.5 million "Texas tower," about one and one-half miles to the southeast.

The ninety-foot-tall Ambrose Light Tower was constructed by Tidewater, Raymond, and Kiewit. It stood on four legs, driven about 190 feet into the sea bottom. The structure was designed to withstand winds of up to 150 miles per hour. The tower was staffed by a crew of six Coast Guardsmen, with four on station at all times.

Transportation to and from the tower was made easier by the presence of a helicopter pad, but life at the station was dreary and sometimes dangerous. The Ambrose Light Tower was automated and destaffed in 1988. After a tanker collided with the tower, the Coast Guard rebuilt it in 1999.

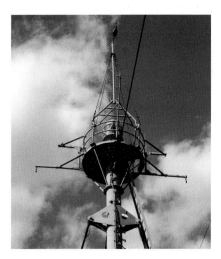

The lightship has two masts topped by lanterns.

The new tower, a three-legged platform surmounted by a solar-powered light, was rammed and badly damaged by a huge Bahamian tanker in November 2007. A lighted buoy was placed about three hundred yards away, and the tower was decommissioned in July 2008.

Meanwhile, the *LV 87*, the original vessel at the site, went on to serve as an examination ship during World War II. It served on the Scotland station, about four and one-half miles west of the Ambrose station, from 1947 to 1962. It was decommissioned in 1964 and donated four years later to the South Street Seaport Museum in New York City.

Today, the *LV 87* is docked at Pier 16 on the East River and is one of several historic vessels opened for tours by the South Street Seaport Museum. Visitors are invited to board the ship to view photographs, charts, and artifacts explaining the historic role of lightships.

The South Street Seaport Museum displays a treasure trove of maritime art and artifacts in a complex of restored nineteenth-century buildings in Lower Manhattan. The area, except for South Street itself, is closed to automobile traffic. The museum's buildings and piers are surrounded by a variety of shops and restaurants.

For directions and other information on visiting South Street Seaport, visit www.southstreetseaportmuseum.org online or call 212-748-8600. The museum's buildings and vessels are easily reached by car or by public transportation.

## SIDE TRIP: *Seaport Marketplace*

The historic buildings and vessels of the South Street Seaport Museum are part of a lively area that includes community space, specialty shops, and food stalls. For more information, visit www.southstreetseaport.com or call 212-SEAPORT.

Circle Line Tours offers scenic cruises leaving from Pier 14 in the Seaport. For information on Circle Line Tours, call 866-925-4631 or visit www.circleline-downtown.com online.

# BLACKWELL ISLAND LIGHTHOUSE

Roosevelt Island, a two-mile-long, narrow island off Manhattan in the East River, was once known as Welfare Island and before that as Blackwell Island. The island had at least three additional names in its early history. The Native Americans called it Minnahanock, and the Dutch, who purchased it in 1637, called it Hog Island. It was briefly called Manning's Island after Captain John Manning.

**Accessibility:** 🚗 🚶

**Geographic coordinates:**
40° 46' 22" N   73° 56' 25" W

**Nearest community:** New York City. Located at the northern end of Roosevelt Island, in the East River.

**Established:** 1872. Present lighthouse built: 1872. Discontinued: 1940s.

**Height of tower:** 50 feet.

After many years of ownership by the Blackwell family, the island was sold to the City of New York in 1828. For many years, it was utilized as a site for prisons, poor houses, and hospitals.

Among the prisoners at the island's Welfare Penitentiary were the politician William "Boss" Tweed, who served a year on corruption-related charges, and the actress Mae West, who was arrested in 1927 for lewd behavior. Mobster Dutch Schultz and blues singer Billie Holliday were also temporary residents of the penitentiary. The famous journalist Nellie Bly went undercover in 1887 to write about the Women's Lunatic Asylum on the island, and her report *Ten Days in a Mad-House* won her wide fame and resulted in many reforms at the hospital.

The federal government did not build the handsome lighthouse at the island's northern tip; the City of New York commissioned it in 1872. Built of gray gneiss stone found on the island, the fifty-foot octagonal tower was designed by James Renwick Jr., who is best remembered for St. Patrick's

Blackwells Island Reef, New York.

**Early 1900s view**

Cathedral. The lighthouse's fixed red light served as an important aid for traffic passing through the narrow channel in the East River. There was never a keeper's house or a resident keeper.

Inmate labor may have been used for its construction, but the lighthouse's origins are shrouded in local legend. According to one story, a resident of the island's asylum named John McCarthy was allowed to build a four-foot-high clay fort on the site shortly before the lighthouse was built, supposedly out of fear of a British attack. McCarthy was encouraged to complete his fort; he was even supplied with Civil War–era cannons.

When the lighthouse was planned, according to legend, McCarthy was persuaded to demolish his fort. Another patient, who called himself "Thomas Maxey, Esq., architect, mason, carpenter, civil engineer, philosopher, and philanthropist," is sometimes said to be the builder of the lighthouse, but McCarthy got the

**Fascinating Fact**

This is a rare example of a nineteenth century lighthouse that was built by a city government, rather than the federal government.

credit on a stone placed at the base of the lighthouse, which read, "This work was done by John McCarthy, who built the lighthouse from the bottom to the top. All ye who do pass by may pray for his soul when he dies." The stone disappeared mysteriously in the 1960s.

The lighthouse served as an aid to navigation for more than seventy years. It was designated a New York City landmark in 1975. Lighthouse Park was created around the tower in 1977, providing panoramic views of Manhattan's Upper East Side, Ward's Island, and the Triborough Bridge. In 1998, an anonymous donation of $120,000 paid for a restoration of the lighthouse.

The island was officially renamed Welfare Island in 1921, then renamed again as Roosevelt Island in 1973. The Roosevelt name came about because of a planned extensive memorial to President Franklin Delano Roosevelt.

In the 1980s and 1990s, Roosevelt Island was developed as a residential community with high-rise apartment buildings conveniently located near the United Nations headquarters on Manhattan's East Side.

To reach Roosevelt Island by car from Manhattan, take the 59th Street Bridge (Upper Level) to 21st Street in Queens. Take 21st Street to 36th Avenue, and turn left onto 36th Ave. Continue to Roosevelt Island via the 36th Avenue Bridge. Turn right on the island and drive to the northern end, where you can park near Lighthouse Park.

From Long Island, take the Central Parkway (West) to the last exit before the Triborough Bridge (Hoyt Avenue) Remain on Hoyt Avenue to 21st Street. Turn left. Continue to 36th Avenue. Take a right turn at 36th Avenue and proceed to Roosevelt Island via the 36th Avenue Bridge.

You can also take the Q or B train to Roosevelt Island, or the Q102 bus. For a real treat, you can access the island via an elevated tramway that leaves from TramPlaza at 59th Street and Second Avenue in Manhattan. The walk to the lighthouse is a bit over a mile from the tramway terminal on the island. The ride, which reaches a height of two hundred fifty feet above the East River, takes you to the island in four minutes. You might recall that the tramway was prominently featured in the movie *Spiderman*.

For more on the Roosevelt Island Tramway, visit www.ny.com/transportation/ri_tramway.html. For more on getting to the island and other information, visit www.rioc.com.

You can also get a good view of the lighthouse from the John Finley Walk in Manhattan near the Gracie Mansion, and from 1st Street in Astoria, Queens. The Circle Line's three-hour "full island" sightseeing cruise passes by; call 212-563-3200 or visit www.circleline42.com online.

# THROGS NECK LIGHT

Throgs Neck, a small peninsula at the junction of the East River and Long Island Sound, is named for John Throckmorton, an Englishman who came to the area in 1643. Throckmorton's settlement lasted only a brief time; it was obliterated by an Indian uprising in which eighteen settlers were killed.

The 1835 tower

**Accessibility:** 🚶 🏛

**Geographic coordinates:**
40° 48' 17" N  73° 47' 27" W

**Nearest community:**
Borough of the Bronx, New York City. Located at the eastern entrance to the East River.

**Established:** 1827.
Present tower built: 1986.
Automated: 1934.

**Height of focal plane:**
60 feet.

**Optics:** Sixth-order Fresnel lens (1855). Fifth-order Fresnel lens (1890). Fourth-order Fresnel lens (1906).

**Characteristic:** Fixed red.

The Throgs Neck community is now part of the New York City borough of the Bronx. Many residents continue to use the old spelling of "Throggs Neck." It's also been corrupted to "Frog's Neck" on occasion.

In March 1821, Congress appropriated $4,000 for a lighthouse at the southern tip of Throgs Neck to mark the entrance to the East River, which leads to New York Harbor. Two additional appropriations totaling $7,500 were needed before construction began in 1826. Land for the station was bought from William Bayard. Timothy, Ezra, and Elisha Daboll built the station's original buildings, which lasted less than a decade.

The light went into service in 1827. The first keeper, Samuel Young, ran a bar at the station that catered primarily to local duck hunters. At least one of Young's successors also sold rum to visitors. It appears that the lighthouse authorities took no action to close down the operation; either nobody told them about it, or they chose to ignore it.

In 1835, the light station buildings were demolished to make room for the construction of Fort Schuyler, named for Major General Philip Schuyler of the Continental Army. Some of the

## SIDE TRIP: *Maritime Industry Museum*

Part of Fort Schuyler at Throgs Neck has been converted into a museum illustrating the history of the United States maritime industry, including commercial shipping, the merchant marine, and the Port of New York. Visitors to the museum enter through fort's sally port and find themselves in the center bastion.

Since the museum's founding in 1986, companies in the maritime industry and merchant marine history buffs have donated objects and artifacts. The museum boasts a large collection of maritime industry books, periodicals, documents, papers, prints, photographs, and old steamship company records.

The museum's hours are Monday through Saturday 9:00 a.m. to 4:00 p.m. Admission and parking are free. For directions and other details, call 718-409-7218 or visit www.sunymaritime.edu online.

stones from the original tower and keeper's dwelling were incorporated into the fort.

A wooden tower and a keeper's house were built alongside the fort in 1835. The lighting apparatus of eleven lamps and reflectors was replaced in 1855 by a sixth-order

Circa 1890s view, with the skeletal tower

Fresnel lens. In the same year, a fog bell was installed. The wooden tower was considered temporary and was found to be leaky and shaky in an 1838 inspection, but it remained in use for more than fifty years. The tower was designed so that it could be easily moved if it was in the way of the fort's guns in a time of emergency.

Throgs Neck had a female keeper, Ellen Lyons, from 1876 to 1881. The badly deteriorated keeper's house was replaced in 1883 by the extant one-and-one-half-story wood-frame dwelling.

Seven years later, a new lighthouse tower was built. The tower was nearly a twin of the lighthouse built in the

same year at Coney Island. The lantern of the sixty-two-foot-tall skeletal cast-iron tower was fitted with a fifth-order Fresnel lens.

With changes in the fort in the early 1900s, the lighthouse was found to be "objectionable from a military point of view," as it stood in the firing path of new five-inch guns. Only sixteen years after it was built, the 1890 tower was replaced by a thirty-foot-tall brick tower with a fourth-order Fresnel lens and was seven hundred feet to the southwest.

Alexander Ferreira, a Civil War veteran and former keeper at the Bergen Point Lighthouse, was keeper from

1884 to 1910. When he died, his son Charles (Charlie) took over as keeper. "When we arrived at the fort," Charlie Ferreira said in an interview years later, "it was still an active army post. They set aside one room next to the soldiers' poolroom as a schoolroom for eight kids on the base. Our teacher was a Private McGloan, who got $2 a month extra on top of his regular pay of $13. All he ever taught us was how to draw the map of South America."

Charlie Ferreira described memorable Fourth of July celebrations in the 1954 interview. "They would fire a salute of forty-four, forty-five guns, however many states we had in the Union at the moment. The smoke was so black you couldn't see a thing. . . . When ex-President Rutherford B. Hayes died in 1893, they shot off twenty-one guns. Heavy guns, too, I guess, because the thunder knocked all the plaster off our cottage walls and broke nineteen windows."

Ferreira also recalled an incident during World War I, while he was keeper. A freighter with no identifying flag cruised past. A shell was fired without proper permission from Fort Totten in Queens. The shot skirted the bow of the ship, skipped off the water, and struck the wall of Fort Schuyler near the lighthouse. Ferreira's wife was making ketchup at the time, and the concussion scattered plaster, glass, and ketchup all over the kitchen.

Fort Schuyler was a popular location for early film crews, who shot movies there with stars such as Gloria Swanson and Charlie Ruggles. Charlie Ferreira was once hired as a stuntman; he had to throw a firebomb into a mockup of a house. Unfortunately, it went off in his hand and caused severe burns.

The brick tower remained in operation until 1934, when a sixty-foot steel skeletal tower was erected. According to some sources, the station was automated at that time, but Charlie Ferreira remained living in the keeper's house until 1944. When he retired that year at the age of seventy, the fort's entire cadet corps of five hundred paraded before him as he stood at attention with his wife, children, grandchildren, and nieces and nephews. Ferreira was presented with a big silver cup as a token of appreciation.

The present square skeletal tower, with its fixed red light sixty feet above the water, dates to 1986. It's the sixth light tower used here in the station's 181-year history.

After Fort Schuyler's decommissioning in 1934, it was converted into the New York Public Nautical School. In 1948, it was incorporated into the State University of New York as State University of New York (SUNY) Maritime College. Today, SUNY Maritime College is an undergraduate and graduate institution focused on engineering, business, science, and maritime transportation. The former keeper's house at the light station now serves as housing for a faculty member.

Throgs Neck is not a destination for anyone in search of photogenic lighthouses; its utilitarian steel tower is decidedly homely. If you do visit, be sure to respect the privacy of the residents of the keeper's house. Don't

## Fascinating Fact

This light stands next to Fort Schuyler, which was a popular shooting location for silent movies starring Gloria Swanson, Charlie Ruggles, and others.

walk onto their property.

To reach SUNY Maritime College from Manhattan, take the North Cross Bronx Expressway east. Follow the Throgs Neck Bridge signs to exit 9 (Harding Ave/Fort Schuyler) just before the bridge. At exit 9, take the left fork, and then make an immediate right onto Harding Avenue. Proceed along Harding Avenue to a stop sign. Turn left on Pennyfield Avenue to the college gatehouse.

After entering the campus, drive about a half-mile on Erben Avenue to a curve in the road, and you'll see the keeper's house and skeletal tower on your left. There are free parking spaces along the road.

# LOST LIGHTS OF NEW YORK HARBOR

## Scotland Lightship

The schooner *Kate Dyer* was about ten miles southwest of Fire Island Lighthouse on Long Island, on its way to New York Harbor when disaster struck in the early evening of December 1, 1866. The steamer *Scotland* accidentally rammed the schooner, which sank quickly, taking the lives of thirteen crewmen.

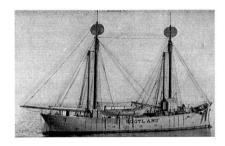

The *LV 7* served at the Scotland station from 1881 to 1902.

Sixteen survivors were taken on board the *Scotland*. The steamer was badly damaged, and the captain decided to try a run for Sandy Hook Bay. In heavy seas, the captain was forced to run the *Scotland* aground on the Outer Middle Bar, about two and one-half miles east/southeast of Sandy Hook Lighthouse. The crew escaped, but much of the steamer's cargo of cheese and beeswax washed ashore at Sandy Hook.

A buoy was placed over the wreck as a warning. Mariners petitioned for something more substantial, and a lightship was put in place in 1868. Until 1891, the station was known officially as the Wreck of Scotland Lightship; it was then changed simply to the Scotland Lightship. A number of vessels served at the station over the years, beginning with the small, wooden-hulled *LV 20*.

The wreck of the *Scotland* was largely demolished with explosives in 1869; the operation was described in the book *Captain Thomas A. Scott, Master Diver* by F. Hopkinson Smith:

> *Captain Scott crawled over every foot of the vessel in his diving dress, made up his mind instantly what to do, bought thirty new wine casks holding sixty gallons each, filled them with powder, sunk and placed each cask himself — some under her lower deck, others back of her boilers — two in the forecastle, five behind her engines — wherever the*

*force would tell, connected the thirty giant bombs by rubber-coated copper wire, twisted the strands into one rope, placed his battery in a rowboat, fell back some hundred yards and made the connection. There was an upheaval, a column of water straight in the air, and the* Scotland *was split like a melon dashed on a sidewalk.*

After the blasting and the removal of the wreck to deeper water, the station was discontinued in 1870. There were complaints from mariners who had come to rely on it, and the lightship was reestablished in 1874.

Between 1892 and 1905, the lightships on the station were rammed by other vessels at least six times. The 104-foot-long wooden-hulled *LV 11* was on the station in January 1909 during a snowstorm when it was rammed by the four-masted schooner *Perry Setzer* carrying a cargo of coal. The *Setzer* suffered more damage than the lightship, and its anchor chain became tangled with one of the lightship's mooring cables.

The steamer *Arapahoe* from Jacksonville, Florida, spotted the lightship's signal flag requesting immediate assistance. The *Arapahoe* was equipped with wireless telegraph equipment, and it put out a call for help. Several vessels, including the lighthouse tender *Larkspur*, were soon on the scene. The *Setzer* was towed to a safe anchorage to ride out the storm.

The last vessel to serve at the Scotland station (1947–62) was the *LV 87*, which had previously spent twenty-four years on the Ambrose station. After its decommissioning, the *LV 87* was subsequently put on display at the South Street Seaport Museum.

The lightship was replaced in 1962 by a large lighted buoy with a fog signal and a radio beacon; a smaller buoy now marks the spot.

## Fascinating Fact

This lightship station took its name from the steamer *Scotland*, which sank on the spot in 1866.

# Bergen Point Light

Bergen Point Light was established in 1849 on a reef at the intersection of the Kill Van Kull and Newark Bay, off the southwestern tip of Bayonne, New Jersey. The contractors George Youngs and William Youngs built both the Bergen Point Lighthouse and the Passaic Lighthouse a few miles away.

The station cost a little under $5,000 to construct. It originally consisted of a two-story wood-frame dwelling with a tower on the center of its roof, topped by an octagonal lantern and built atop a caisson sixty feet in diameter. The light went into service on September 20, 1849, the same day as the Passaic Light five miles to the north.

Just four years after the light went into service, Major W. D. Fraser of the Corps of Engineers reported that it was in a bad state:

> The wharf rises about six feet above high-water mark, and is in a very precarious condition, being constructed of very light stuff, and negligently framed. The house is settled at the center, causing great injury to the ceilings both in the hall and upper rooms . . . The dwelling-house is sufficiently commodious, but its condition, as well as that of the wharf, is too bad to justify

**Geographic coordinates:**
40° 38' 32" N  74° 08' 41" W

**Nearest community:** Bayonne, New Jersey. Located in Newark Bay, at the entrance to the Kill Van Kull.

**Established:** 1849. Discontinued: ca. 1948.

**Height of focal plane (1863):** 53 feet.

**Optics:** Sixth-order Fresnel lens (1855). Fourth-order Fresnel lens (1904).

**Fog signal:** Bell with striking machinery (1873).

The 1859 lighthouse

*me in asking anything for their repairs. The whole work ought to be renewed, and something better substituted in its place.*

Fraser suggested an appropriation of $20,000 for the rebuilding of the station. It took three years, but Congress appropriated that amount in August 1856. Work on a new lighthouse began in 1857, and the new combined lighthouse and dwelling was completed in 1859. A forty-one-foot-tall square stone tower stood at the corner of a two-story dwelling.

A sixth-order Fresnel lens, probably the one that had been in use in the old lighthouse since 1855, was installed. The optic was upgraded to a fourth-order Fresnel lens in 1904. The station also had a fog bell, at first rung by hand. Striking

---

## Fascinating Fact

The first (1849) lighthouse at this location was so badly built that it lasted only a decade.

---

machinery was installed in 1873.

The first keeper of the new lighthouse was Peter Girth, who came to the station in 1853. He was followed in 1863 by John MacDonald, who served a decade at a yearly salary of $400 before his death in 1873. Hannah MacDonald, John's widow, was appointed to succeed her husband. She remained keeper until 1879. She was succeeded by her son, John H. MacDonald, who stayed until 1881.

Robert Gray (reported in some sources as Robert Ray), a native of Ireland, became keeper in January 1902. About three weeks later, he left to row ashore for supplies, leaving his aunt and her three sons at the lighthouse. When Gray didn't return, the flag at the lighthouse was flown upside down as a signal of distress.

It took nine days before help arrived. Frederick Lumbreyer of Bayonne, a former policeman, took his boat through the thick ice to the lighthouse. When he arrived with provisions, Gray's aunt and her children had been out of food for two days.

They had kept the light burning each night through the whole ordeal. Gray was presumed drowned. His aunt served as interim keeper until August Kjelberg was appointed at the end of March.

John R. Carlsson, a veteran of six years on the Sandy Hook Lightship, was appointed keeper in 1906. Carlsson was credited in 1913 with the rescue of a boy from a capsized skiff in the Kill Van Kull, but the boy's companion was lost.

Life at the station was a welcome change for Carlsson and his wife, Anna, who moved into the lighthouse with their daughter, Annie. Young Annie made the newspapers as the daring keeper's daughter who rowed to shore each day, never allowing the wind or tides to keep her from attending school.

Hans Beuthe, originally from Germany, served as keeper from 1921 to 1941. With the dredging and widening of the channel in the Kill Van Kull in the 1940s, the lighthouse was demolished.

## Passaic Light

The first lighthouse here was a twin of the original Bergen Point Light, and both stations were established in 1849. The Passaic Light came about largely because of the urging of Michael Nerney, a local harbor pilot and former sea captain. Nerney convinced Congressman Dudley S. Gregory of Jersey City of the need for the lighthouse, and $6,000 was appropriated by Congress in 1847.

The Passaic Light warned mariners of shallow mud flats on the west side of the channel in Newark Bay, about a mile south of the entrance to the Passaic River and about five miles

---

**Geographic coordinates:**
40° 41' 44" N  74° 07' 40" W

**Nearest community:** Newark, New Jersey. Located in Newark Bay, near the entrances to the Passaic and Hackensack rivers.

**Established:** 1849. Discontinued: 1914.

**Height of focal plane (1863):** 51 feet.

**Optics:** Sixth-order Fresnel lens (1853). Fifth-order Fresnel lens (1894). Fourth-order Fresnel lens (1907).

**Fog signal:** Bell with striking machinery (1891).

north of Bergen Point. The lighthouse stood offshore, but its former location is now on solid ground in the city of Newark.

The original station consisted of a wooden tower on the roof of two-story wood-frame dwelling that stood atop a wharf that reached six feet above high water. The lantern originally

## Fascinating Fact

Eliza MacCashin lived at this station for thirty-three years (1881–1914), as assistant keeper and later as principal keeper.

**The 1859 lighthouse**

held a sixth-order lens showing a fixed white light. The first keeper was Michael Nerney, whose agitation had helped secure the funding for the station. The light went into service on September 20, 1849.

Like the first Bergen Point Lighthouse, the building was so poorly constructed that it had to be rebuilt within a decade. The 1859 lighthouse was a square tower built at the corner of a two-and-one-half-story keeper's dwelling, constructed on a substantial new stone pier.

Nerney remained keeper for twenty-one years. He kept track of the passing vessels, recording as many as three hundred in a single day. When Nerney was removed from his position, he blamed politics; he had strongly opposed the building of a bridge across Newark Bay.

Over the years, several wives of the principal keepers served in the position of assistant keeper. Dennis MacCashin (sometimes spelled Mac-Cashian or McCashin) became keeper in 1881, and his wife, Eliza, was the assistant keeper for twenty-two years. Dennis MacCashin died in 1903, and Eliza MacCashin won the appointment to succeed him as keeper. Her salary in 1908 was $600 yearly.

Eliza MacCashin, who was the second cousin of President William McKinley, kept the station for the next eleven years with the help of her son, Hugh O. MacCashin. The MacCashins also tended a stake light called the Elbow Beacon, to the north on a shoal near the entrance to the Passaic River.

The light lost its importance over the years as the channel shifted. Four small acetylene-powered lights went into service, and the lighthouse was deactivated in 1914.

Eliza MacCashin died in 1914. Hugh MacCashin remained living in the lighthouse until 1933; he was paid $1 yearly as custodian. Once, when a reporter wanted to interview him, Hugh MacCashin asked why anyone would want to read about a "lighthouse keeper without a light." The building was demolished many years ago.

## North Brother Island Light

As early as 1829, authorities recognized the need for a lighthouse in the East River north of the treacherous channel known as Hell Gate. North Brother Island, in the small Bay of Brothers near Rikers Island, was an ideal location. Congress appropriated $5,000 for the station, but the owner of the land refused to sell, and the project was shelved.

In 1848, after another appropriation of $10,000, the owner asked the exorbitant price of $5,000 for two acres of land, and again the project was delayed. The State of New York finally intervened in 1868 after a third congressional appropriation

**Geographic coordinates:**
40° 47' 57" N  73° 53' 59" W

**Nearest community:** Borough of the Bronx, New York City. Located in Bay of Brothers, East River.

**Established:** 1869. Discontinued: 1953.

**Height of focal plane (1873):** 50 feet.

**Optics:** Sixth-order Fresnel lens (1869). Fourth-order Fresnel lens (1900).

**Fog signal:** Bell with striking machinery, one blow every 15 seconds (1889).

of $7,500. The government secured the land, and the lighthouse was completed by the end of 1869.

The lighthouse took the form of a dwelling with the lighthouse tower at the front end of its mansard roof. It was a style in vogue at the time; similar structures were built at Rose Island and Pomham Rocks in Rhode Island, Esopus Meadows in New York, and Colchester Reef in Vermont, among other locations. The light was fifty feet above mean high water with a sixth-order Fresnel lens showing a fixed white light.

Joseph D. Meade became keeper in October 1902. During the following January, Meade left to visit his mother in the city, leaving his two brothers to keep an eye on the station. Two days later, Meade had not arrived at his mother's house and had not returned to the island, and the police were called. His boat was found at a city

North Brother Island Light

dock, but Meade's body was never found, and the mystery surrounding his disappearance was never solved.

The City of New York moved the Riverside City Hospital for Contagious Diseases to North Brother Island in 1885. The hospital was converted into a drug rehabilitation facility in the 1950s, and it closed in the early 1960s.

The island is also famous for a monumental shipping disaster, the June 1904 fire on the steamer *General Slocum* that killed more than a thousand people on the East River. The ship eventually went aground at North Brother, and the staff and patients from Riverside Hospital were instrumental in saving many passengers.

William Murray, a Brooklyn native who had sailed to China at the age of sixteen on the crew of a ship, became keeper in 1930. The keeper's duties at North

## Fascinating Fact

North Brother Island's most famous resident for many years was Mary Mallon, better known as "Typhoid Mary."

Brother at the time included looking after six smaller acetylene gas-powered lights in the vicinity, referred to locally as "bug lights." Murray's son Tom often accompanied his father on work trips to these lights. "It was kind of a hairy job in winter," he remembered later, "particularly going into Hell's Gate."

By the time he was fifteen or sixteen, Tom Murray was tending the bug lights by himself. "You had to nose up to the riprap at the lights," he said in a 2004 interview. "You had to swing a rope and catch one of the legs of the lights and pull yourself up."

**Keeper William J. Murray with his daughter Lillian in the 1930s**

Landing or launching the boat at North Brother Island wasn't always so easy, either. "One time the boat got away, and I had to swim after it," Tom remembered.

Travel by boat could be hazardous in certain parts of the harbor. "Once we were passing Rikers Prison," Tom recalled, "and somebody on the island fired a shot, and we heard the whiz of the bullet. My father had a hunch it was the warden's son. You weren't supposed to go too close, and we gave it a wide berth after that!"

Tom Murray had a Scotch terrier at the light station, and one of his brothers also had a dog and a guinea pig. There were specific rules about where the lighthouse kids could go on the island. "We were on the tip of the island, fenced off," said Tom. "There was a hospital there. We used to get chased by the head doctor, and he'd tell us to get back."

Tom Murray traveled from North Brother Island by ferry and trolley car to the city for school. The ferry crew would sometimes let Tom or his brother steer the vessel.

Probably North Brother's most famous resident was Mary Mallon, better known as "Typhoid Mary." In 1906, wealthy New York banker Charles Henry Warren employed Mallon as a cook. Six of the eleven people living in the Warren household became ill with typhoid, and the outbreak was traced to Mallon.

She was also blamed for typhoid among seven of the eight families for whom she had previously worked. The New York City Health Department eventually quarantined her in a cottage on the grounds of the hospital on North Brother Island, and she remained there until her death in 1938.

To young Tom Murray, Typhoid Mary was just another island neighbor. "I'd pass her going to the ferry, and she'd give me an apple or an orange, and I'd take them to be polite," he said.

Tom Murray left his lighthouse home in 1944 to enter the navy, and his father retired as keeper two years later. A Coast Guard crew ran the

North Brother Island Light Station after the Murrays left. In 1953, the lighthouse was decommissioned, and an automatic light was installed on the nearby fog bell tower. A buoy near the island eventually replaced the light.

According to Tom Murray, it wasn't long before everything that could be taken from the lighthouse was gone. One piece of the old light station was salvaged—the fog bell was refurbished and is on display at the New York City Police Department's Harbor Unit at College Point. The bell serves as a memorial to the unit's police officers who have died in the line of duty.

Today the tower has collapsed, and the rest of the building has crumbled. It can safely be considered a lost lighthouse, beyond hope of restoration. Along with neighboring South Brother Island, North Brother is protected today as a bird sanctuary. The island is closed to the public, but you may get a view from Randalls Island in Manhattan; take the Randalls Island exit from the Triborough Bridge.

## Hell Gate Light

The strong currents and hidden dangers in the narrow passage in the East River known as Hell Gate (sometimes referred to euphemistically as "Hurl Gate") were scourges to mariners for many years. Historians say the name comes from the Dutch "hellegat," meaning an open channel, but it's a fitting name in any case.

It's estimated that as many as one thousand wrecks still lie in the waters of Hell Gate. The passage made an impression on Charles Dickens, who wrote that he viewed "Hell Gate, Frying Pan, Hog's Back, and other notorious localities" from shipboard during an 1842 visit to New York.

In the early days, many vessels met their doom when they struck Pot

**Geographic coordinates:**
40° 46' 42" N  73° 56' 06" W

**Nearest community:** Borough of Queens, New York City. Located at Hallets Point in Hell Gate Passage, East River.

**Established:** 1884.

**Height of tower (1884):** 255 feet.

**Optics:** Nine electric arc lights (1884).

**Comtemporary illustration of the 1884 Hell Gate Light**

Rock, a small but menacing ledge just below the surface. During an 1848 survey, there were eight wrecks in a single day, and it was estimated that one in fifty vessels sustained injury when passing through the channel. The blasting of Pot Rock and other obstructions in the early 1850s helped, but Hell Gate was still a menace for large ships.

More blasting followed, most notably at Flood Rock off Hallets Point in October 1885. A large crowd gathered for the event, and the blast was heard forty miles away at West Point. The work doubled the width of the channel to twelve hundred feet.

In 1884, a new light was established at Hallets Point, which jutted out into the east side of the passage from the Astoria neighborhood of Queens. Established after a congressional appropriation of $20,000 in 1882, the Hell Gate Light was an expensive experiment. It was the tallest iron skeletal light tower built to that time, at 255 feet. Its nine electric arc lamps produced a light that was said to rival the full moon. Although it wasn't a traditional lighthouse, it can be called the first electric lighthouse in the United States. The light went into service on October 20, 1884.

By early 1886, keeper Daniel Fox reported that the boilers for the electric plant frequently malfunctioned. There were also problems with the light being too bright; it blinded mariners and cast harsh and misleading shadows. There was also a snag involving the owner of the land. The government had leased, rather than bought, the property, and the lease had run out.

## Fascinating Fact

The skeletal tower in use here 1884–88 was the first electric lighthouse in the United States.

The electric light was turned off in 1888, and the tower was dismantled; the surplus materials were sold at auction. A wooden combined lighthouse and fog bell tower was subsequently built at Hallets Point.

Accidents in Hell Gate continued in spite of the light and fog signal. One of the more dramatic wrecks occurred on July 1, 1894, when the steam yacht *Aztec* from a local yacht club was run down by the excursion steamer *Sam Sloan*. Nearly ten feet of the yacht's stern was cut off, and the boat was dashed up onto the rocks in front of the lighthouse. The eight people on board were all able to get safely ashore. Arthur Donnelly, the keeper at the lighthouse, agreed with other witnesses that the pilot of the *Sam Sloan* was at fault.

A few months later, on February 9, 1895, a ferry headed for Astoria with a large number of passengers became disabled in drifting ice in the passage. A tugboat caught up with the ferry off North Brother Island and towed it to port. During the same night, Keeper Donnelly reported a canal boat drifting helplessly past in the ice-clogged channel.

The wooden lighthouse was eventually replaced by a black skeleton tower with a light thirty-five feet above the water. That structure was later replaced by a simple post light in the vicinity of Hellgate Field, an athletic facility.

**Hell Gate Light in the early 1900s**

# PART TWO
# The Historic Hudson

From its early exploration to pivotal battles in the American Revolution, and from the writings of Washington Irving and James Fenimore Cooper to the romantic vision of the Hudson River School of artists, the Hudson River occupies a prominent place in our national history, arts, and mythology.

The river—315 miles in total length and navigable for 150 miles—begins at Lake Tear of the Clouds in the Adirondack Mountains, and it empties at the spacious New York Harbor between the New Jersey Palisades and Manhattan. Below the city of Troy, New York, the river is a tidal estuary. Its widest point is at the Tappan Zee Bridge, where 3.5 miles of water separate Nyack and Tarrytown. The river's expansive basin, 13,400 square miles in area, extends from New York into parts of Vermont, Massachusetts, Connecticut, and New Jersey.

For at least 7,000 years, the area was home to the Algonquin people, who called the river "Mohicanituk," meaning "river that flows both ways." According to some historians, these people bent trees along the banks of the river and lit signal fires to help mark and find their way.

The Hudson was the first significant river encountered by European explorers. French fur traders were among the earliest visitors. The Florentine navigator Giovanni da Verrazzano, searching for a passage to Asia, explored the river aboard *La Dauphine* in 1524.

Verrazzano described spacious New York Harbor in his report to King Francis I as "a very agreeable situation located within two small prominent hills, in the midst of which flowed to the sea a very big river, which was deep within the mouth: and from sea to the hills of that [place] with the rising of the tides, which we found eight feet, any laden ship might have passed."

In 1608, the Dutch East India Company hired the English trader Henry Hudson to find a shortcut to the Orient. Hudson left Amsterdam

Jeffrey's Hook Light

in April 1609 with an eighty-ton ship, the *Half Moon*, and a crew of twenty Dutch and English sailors.

After a troubled voyage across the Atlantic that included threats of mutiny and a violent storm that toppled the mainmast, the *Half Moon* sailed as far south as Chesapeake Bay before heading north. The expedition passed Manhattan and entered the river on September 12, 1609. "The land grew very high and mountainous; the river is full of fish," wrote Robert Juet, an officer who kept a journal of the voyage.

Hudson sailed up and down the river for about three weeks. He called it "River of Mountains" and declared the region "as pleasant a land as one can tread upon." These sentiments masked Hudson's disappointment at not finding a passage to Asia.

A year later, on his final attempt to find the elusive passage, Hudson sailed north to what we now know as Hudson Bay. Forced to winter over in James Bay, the crew mutinied and set Hudson, his son, and other officers adrift. They were never seen again.

Although Hudson failed to achieve his goals, his explorations had enormous impact. Descriptions of a sweet smelling land with abundant trees, fine soil for cultivation, and fur-bearing animals for trapping drew wide attention. The Dutch claimed the Hudson River Valley and formed the West India Company to oversee Dutch ventures in the New World. In the 1620s, New Amsterdam was established at present-day Manhattan.

Settlements spread northward along the Hudson River, and by 1664 the New Netherland colony had almost 9,000 inhabitants. In that year, a British fleet conquered the Dutch colony without much of a struggle, and New York was born. The Dutch influence may still be found in the folklife and architecture of much of the region.

A new era for American navigation dawned in August 1807, when the inventor Robert Fulton piloted his steamboat, the *Clermont*, up the Hudson. It took the revolutionary vessel thirty-two hours to steam to Albany.

Whether it was the first successful demonstration of a steam-powered vessel is disputed, but there's no doubt that Fulton was the first to put the technology to practical use. The success of the *Clermont* as a packet boat on the river led to the rapid proliferation of steamboats built by Fulton and others. Within fifty years, steam travel on America's rivers was a way of life.

The next important leap in commerce on the Hudson River came about largely through the efforts of Dewitt Clinton, who, as New York City mayor and later as the state's governor, threw his political weight behind the construction of what some nicknamed "Clinton's Big Ditch." In 1825, the Erie Canal connected the Hudson River to the Great Lakes. This marvel of engineering, 363 miles in length, joined the eastern end of Lake Erie at Buffalo to the Hudson River at Albany.

The new waterway's impact was huge, as it instantly made New York the leading commercial port of the nation and spurred westward movement of settlers. Before the canal, the Allegheny Mountains represented the nation's western frontier.

The Delaware and Hudson Canal, which connected the Delaware River to the Hudson River in 1828, provided a route for the transportation of coal from mines in Pennsylvania to New York City. The canal system was expanded in 1903 with the development of the New York State Barge Canal system, including the addition of three branches to the Erie Canal: the Champlain, the Oswego, and the Cayuga and Seneca Canals.

Before the Erie Canal, the navigational aids on the river were haphazard, with small lanterns hung here and there along the shore. With flourishing commerce came the need for improved aids to navigation, and the federal government met the challenge. By 1895, there were forty-eight aids to navigation from New York

Tarrytown Light and the Tappan Zee Bridge

City to Troy. Most were simple post lights; the first lighthouse was established at Stony Point in 1826.

This book contains information on fourteen lighthouses, of which only seven remain. The seven proud survivors stand as witnesses to the great age of maritime commerce on the Hudson River. They are also a testament to the indomitable men and women who have rescued them from the scrap heap.

Also included in this part is a chapter on the Statue of Liberty, which stands close to the entrance to the Hudson. It's known primarily as one of the nation's most enduring monuments, but "Liberty Enlightning the World" did serve as a lighthouse for some years early in its history.

# Hudson River Lights

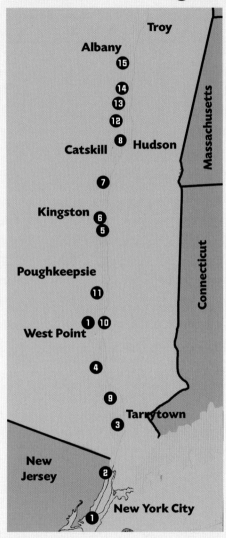

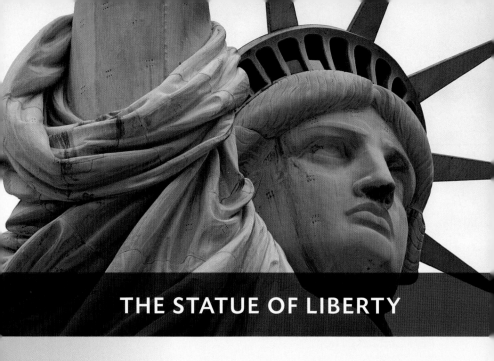

# THE STATUE OF LIBERTY

**Accessibility:** 🚗 ⛵

**Geographic coordinates:**
40° 41' 21" N  74° 02' 40" W

**Nearest city:** Jersey City, New Jersey. Located on Liberty Island, New York Harbor, about a half-mile from Jersey City, just south of the mouth of the Hudson River.

**Established:** 1886. Discontinued as an aid to navigation: 1902.

**Height (including base):** 291 feet.

**Height (statue only):** 151 feet.

The lighthouse is universally recognized as a symbol of strength, hope, and faith, so it's fitting that the Statue of Liberty, one of our most beloved symbols of democracy and freedom, also served as a lighthouse in its early years.

Head of Statue of Liberty on display in park in Paris

Located on twelve-acre Bedloe's Island (now known as Liberty Island) in New York Harbor, just south of the entrance to the Hudson River, the "Statue of Liberty Enlightening the World" was a gift of friendship from the people of France to the people of the United States. The statue's beginnings go back to 1871, when the sculptor Frederic-Auguste Bartholdi traveled to New York Harbor. He wrote of how the visit inspired him:

> *The picture that is presented to the view when one arrives at New York is marvelous: when—after some days of voyaging—in the pearly radiance of a beautiful morning is revealed the magnificent spectacle of those immense cities, of those rivers extending as far as the eye can reach, festooned with masts and flags . . . it is thrilling . . . . Yes, in this very place shall be raised the statue of Liberty, as grand as the idea which it embodies . . . .*

From its conception, Bartholdi's statue was envisioned as a combined monument and lighthouse, and early

**Early 1900s postcard**

articles on the statue described powerful electric lights that would be installed in the torch and/or diadem (crown).

A lack of funding delayed the project for some years. The statue was completed in 1884 and shipped to New York in June 1885. Alexandre-Gustave Eiffel, of Eiffel Tower fame, designed the iron pylon and skeletal framework for the statue.

**Fascinating Fact**

The statue originally served as an official aid to navigation; the U.S. Lighthouse Board managed it from 1886 to 1901.

The pedestal, designed and funded in the United States, was completed inside the walls of star-shaped Fort Wood in 1886.

The statue was placed on the pedestal, and a dedication took place on October 28, 1886, as President Grover Cleveland accepted the statue on behalf of the United States. Lady Liberty stands 151 feet tall from her base to the tip of her torch, and 291 feet from the base of the foundation to the torch, which is 305 feet above sea level. The weight of the copper statue is 260 tons.

President Cleveland ordered that the statue be "maintained, lighted, and tended in accordance with such rules and regulations as now exist" under the U. S. Lighthouse Board.

Lighting the statue was one of the most unusual challenges the Lighthouse Board would ever face.

Because of inclement weather on the day of the dedication, the statue's first lighting took place four days later, on November 1, 1886. It was the first lighthouse in the nation to be powered by electricity, but the initial results were disappointing: the pedestal was well lighted, but most of the statue remained in darkness. The press unmercifully compared the disembodied light in the torch, shown through a double row of circular openings in the base of the flame, to a glow-worm.

The lighting dilemma was solved with the installation of five arc lamps backed by parabolic reflectors, placed inside the walls of Fort Wood and aimed upward at the statue. The system was the invention of James J. Wood, an electrician for the American Electric Manufacturing Company.

The American Electric Manufacturing Company donated the cost of the lighting apparatus and the power

## SIDE TRIP: *Ellis Island Immigration Museum*

The ferries from Battery Park in New York City and from Liberty State Park in New Jersey, in addition to providing access to the Statue of Liberty, also stop at the Ellis Island Immigration Museum. The museum, in the beautifully restored 27.5-acre immigration complex, tells the moving story of the twelve million immigrants who entered the United States through its doors. The museum includes the American Family Immigration History Center, the American Immigrant Wall of Honor (with more than 700,000 names), and the Ellis Island Living Theater.
**For more information, visit www. ellisisland.org online. For ticket rates and availability and schedule information, call (877) LADY TIX or (877) 523-9849 or visit www. statuecruises.com.**

plant to run it only until November 6. They were persuaded to allow the lights to stay on for one more night so that Frederic-Auguste Bartholdi could view it for himself. Bartholdi was pleased, calling the lighting of the torch "happy in effect." The statue went dark for a brief time, but the Lighthouse Board

**The arm and torch on display at the Philadelphia Centennial Exhibition in 1876**

swiftly completed an engine house, and the lighting system was back in operation on November 22.

Just after Christmas 1886, a keeper, A. E. Littlefield, was put in charge of the lighting equipment at a yearly salary of $1,000. In the ensuing years, the station had as many as four assistants assigned along with the principal keeper. A three-story brick building on the island, formerly used as a hospital, was converted into a dwelling for the keepers and their families.

Better, more permanent, equipment was needed, and Congress

## SIDE TRIP: *Liberty State Park*

If you visit the Statue of Liberty from the New Jersey side, your departure point is 1,212-acre Liberty State Park in Jersey City. The park offers good views of New York City's skyline and wide expanses of open space, an interpretive center, picnic areas, and a marina. Adjacent to the interpretive center is a 36-acre marsh known as the Richard J. Sullivan Natural Area; it's one of the last remaining tidal marshes of the Hudson River estuary. A self-guided nature trail leads through the marsh.

The park is also home to the Liberty Science Center, a family science center with three floors of interactive exhibits and the Kodak Omnimax Theatre. The Liberty Walk Promenade on the park's eastern edge offers views of the Statue of Liberty, about 2,000 feet away. **For more information, visit www.libertystatepark.org or www.state.nj.us/dep/parksandforests/, or call (201) 915-3440.**

appropriated $19,500 (of a requested $32,500) toward that purpose in 1887. Over the next two years, a new steam plant was built, as well as a cistern, a coalhouse, and a new engine and boiler house.

A brief experiment was tried beginning in October 1892, with red, white, and blue lights installed in the diadem. The idea of painting the statue white or gilding it, in an effort to improve its nighttime visibility, was discussed but never implemented.

The marriage of the Lighthouse Board and Lady Liberty was a rocky one. The facility was expensive to maintain, and Congress was stingy with appropriations. The statue was never regarded as an important aid to navigation; in fact, in 1889 it didn't even appear on the official light list as a New York Harbor light.

The Lighthouse Board gladly turned over its jurisdiction of the statue to the War Department in November 1901. On March 1, 1902, it was officially discontinued as an aid to navigation. Authority over

---

### SIDE TRIP:
### Battery Park

If you're visiting the Statue of Liberty from New York City, you'll catch the ferry at Battery Park, a twenty-five-acre park at the southern tip of Manhattan that's named for an artillery battery once located there. The park's Castle Garden, originally built as a fort in anticipation of the War of 1812, became the world's first immigrant depot in 1855. There are extensive gardens in the park; the Gardens of Remembrance, with native grasses and flowering perennials, pay tribute to those who died on September 11, 2001. The park is also home to the Battery Gardens Restaurant, offering sweeping views of New York Harbor.
**For more information, visit www.thebattery.org or www.nycgovparks.org, or call (212) NEW-YORK.**

---

the statue eventually passed to the National Park Service in the 1930s.

You may visit the Statue of Liberty via ferry from Liberty State Park in Jersey City, New Jersey, or from Battery Park in New York City. For more information, visit www.nps.gov/stli/ online or call (212) 363-3200.

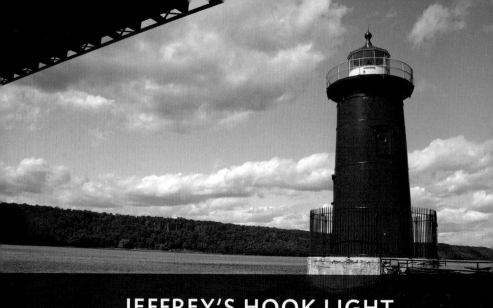

# JEFFREY'S HOOK LIGHT

**Accessibility:** 🚗 🚶

**Geographic coordinates:** 40° 51' 01" N  73° 56' 49" W

**Nearest city:** New York City. Located near the end of the George Washington Bridge in Fort Washington Park, east side of the Hudson River.

**Established:** 1889 (post light).

**Present lighthouse built:** 1880 (originally served as Sandy Hook North Beacon, NJ). Deactivated: 1948. Relighted: 2002. Tower moved to present site: 1921.

**Height of tower:** 40 feet.

**Height of focal plane:** 61 feet.

**Previous optic:** Fifth-order Fresnel lens.

**Present optic:** 300 mm.

**Characteristic:** White light; one second on, two seconds off.

The original life span of this lighthouse as an aid to navigation, which lasted only from 1921 to 1947 in its present location, is of little significance in comparison to the warm place it occupies in the hearts of generations of children. Devoted lighthouse buffs might know it by its proper name, but to most people, this is the beloved Little Red Lighthouse in the shadow of the Great Gray Bridge.

The point of land known as Jeffrey's Hook is on the west side of Manhattan Island, on the east shore of the Hudson River and about twelve miles north of Upper New York Bay. The present lighthouse site was on the perimeter of Fort Washington during the American Revolution, established along with Fort Lee on the New Jersey side of the Hudson. Much of the land along the riverbank in the vicinity of Jeffrey's Hook was acquired by the City of New York in 1896, and it became Fort Washington Park.

As shipping traffic increased in the vicinity in the late nineteenth century, a navigational light was needed to help warn mariners away from a treacherous reef near Jeffrey's Hook. In 1889, a twenty-foot-tall red stake was erected with two red lanterns, one hanging ten feet above the other. The lights were intensified in 1895, but the ten-candlepower lights remained insufficient.

In its 1896 and 1897 annual reports, the Lighthouse Board made a case for something more substantial:

## Fascinating Fact

Letters from children helped save the "Little Red Lighthouse" in the late 1940s.

*A larger light and fog bell here would be valuable aids to navigation. The point extends well out into the river, with deep water close to its outer end. The usual route of steamers passing up and down the river is close to the point. The present post light should be replaced by a new structure upon which should be the lantern with the bell below.*

In 1897, it was announced that permission had been acquired from New York City's parks department to establish a lighthouse and fog signal at Jeffrey's Hook, and an appropriation of $1,400 was requested to erect the structures. The funds were not immediately forthcoming, so the request was repeated yearly through 1907. By that time, the estimated cost had risen to $3,400.

It took more than another decade before action was finally taken, prompted by the development of the New York State Barge Canal system and the deep Hudson Shipway. In 1918, officials of the Bureau of Lighthouses decided that an extant lighthouse tower, built in 1880 and previously in use as the North Beacon at Sandy Hook in New Jersey, would be relocated to Jeffrey's Hook.

The 1880 lighthouse was a conical cast-iron tower typical of many built in the 1870s and 1880s, mostly in the Northeast. It had been in storage at Staten Island, New York, since 1917.

A letter from an official at the lighthouse depot at Staten Island in June 1918 stated: "It is proposed to erect this tower on a concrete base on the ledge at the point where the present Jeffrey's Hook Light is located, a fog bell to be bracketed to the outside of tower with all operating mechanism inside the tower, the light to be a flashing red acetylene light." New York City's parks department soon gave permission for the placement of the lighthouse on city property.

On October 10, 1921, the tower was reassembled in its present location. In its former location, the lighthouse was fifty-five feet tall. A section of the original structure was left out in the new location, making the height of the reassembled lighthouse forty feet. The characteristic was a one-second red flash alternating with

## SIDE TRIP:
### Fort Washington Park

Jeffrey's Hook Lighthouse is located in this 160-acre park, named for a five-bastion fort constructed here in 1776. British and Hessian forces captured the fort in November 1776 as General George Washington watched from Fort Lee on the New Jersey side of the Hudson River. After the war, the fort disappeared, but the area was named Washington Heights. The park now features baseball fields, basketball courts, tennis courts, and a playground. One of the park's most popular events is the annual Little Red Lighthouse Festival, held in September.

**For more information, see www.nycgovparks.org or call (212) 304–2365.**

a two-second eclipse, with a focal plane height of sixty-one feet above the water.

A 1,000-pound fog bell was mounted on the lower part of the lighthouse. A local care-taker or "lamplighter" wound the clock-work mechanisms that sounded the bell and rotated the lens.

A 1926 article in the *New York Times* described the daily duties of the

**Early view of the lighthouse in its present location**

lamplighter, William Knapp. He vis-ited the lighthouse in the evening to turn the acetylene gas-powered light on, and he returned in the morning to turn it off. In times of fog, he vis-ited the lighthouse every few hours to wind the mechanism that sounded the fog bell every fifteen seconds.

The massive George Washing-ton Bridge was completed in 1931. The suspension bridge spans the river from the sites of Fort Washington on

the New York side to Fort Lee on the New Jersey side. For a time during construction, the lighthouse tower was temporarily relocated; it was returned and placed on a new foun-dation when the work was completed. The $60 million bridge was dedicated on October 24, 1931, with more than 30,000 citizens of New York and New Jersey on hand.

At the time of its dedication, the bridge had the longest main span in the world at 3,500 feet; its over-all length is 4,760 feet, and it rises some 600 feet above the river. In the first year of the bridge's existence, 5,509,900 vehicles passed across. By 2005, the number grew to more than 107 million vehicles.

The bright lights of the bridge rendered the lighthouse virtually obsolete. It was still in operation in 1942 when Hildegarde Swift and Lynd Ward wrote the popular children's book *The Little Red Lighthouse and the Great Gray Bridge*. The book told a tale of loss and

The spiral stairway inside Jeffrey's Hook Light

recovery of self-worth that children and adults could easily appreciate.

In the beginning of the book, the lighthouse is proud of its role in navigation: "It felt big and useful and important. 'What would the boats do without me?' it thought." When the bridge is completed in the story, the lighthouse is left feeling small and insignificant. But one foggy night, the bridge tells the lighthouse that its light and bell are still needed, that it is still "the master of the river." The lighthouse calls, "Look out! Danger! Watch me!" Its place in the world was secured.

Despite the popular book and public affection for the lighthouse, the Coast Guard decommissioned it in 1948. The lamp was extinguished, seemingly for good. When plans were announced to auction the lighthouse, a flood of letters from fans of the children's book and other concerned citizens convinced the government to make other plans.

On July 23, 1951, the lighthouse was given to the City of New York. The tower was allowed to fall into disrepair until a $209,000 restoration was carried out in 1986. The work included reconstruction of the tower's concrete foundation and the installation of new steel doors.

Some painting and renovation was completed in 2000 by PRE-SERV, a company specializing in historic properties. New electric lines and interior lighting were installed. In 2002, a 300-millimeter lens was installed, and the lighthouse was relit as a private aid to navigation.

The relighting came at the annual Little Red Lighthouse Festival on September 19, 2002, with about 7,000 well-wishers on hand. The celebrity readers of *The Little Red Lighthouse and the Great Gray Bridge* at the event were actor James Earl Jones and author Carol Higgins Clark.

The lighthouse's most recent face-lift came in 2007, thanks to a $45,000 gift from the paint manufacturer Benjamin Moore. A fresh coat of bright red paint was applied, new lantern glass was installed, and general repairs were completed. The project was celebrated at the fifteenth annual Little Red Lighthouse Festival, when TV sex therapist Dr. Ruth Westheimer joined parks commissioner Adrian Benepe in a reading of *The Little Red Lighthouse and the Great Gray Bridge.*

The only lighthouse on Manhattan Island may be reached by driving or taking the "A" train to West 181st Street. Walk west on 181st Street toward the river, cross a pedestrian footbridge, and follow the path to Fort Washington Park and the lighthouse.

Commuters can see the lighthouse from parts of Riverside Drive and the Henry Hudson Parkway. It may also be seen from the Palisades Interstate Park between Edgewater and Englewood Cliffs, New Jersey.

City park rangers lead school tours and conduct tours of the lighthouse for the public on occasion in summer. For the schedule and more information, call (212) 304–2365, or write to Urban Park Rangers, Inwood Hill Park, 1234 Fifth Ave., first floor, New York, NY 10029.

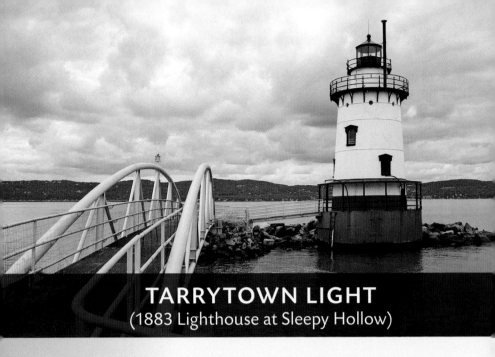

# TARRYTOWN LIGHT
## (1883 Lighthouse at Sleepy Hollow)

**Accessibility:**

**Geographic coordinates:**
41° 05' 03" N  73° 52' 27" W

**Nearest community:**
Village of Sleepy Hollow. Located a short distance offshore near Kingsland Point Park, on the east side of the Hudson River, about one mile north of the Tappan Zee Bridge.

**Established:** 1883.

**Present lighthouse built:**
1883. Automated: 1959. Deactivated: 1961.

**Height of focal plane:**
56 feet.

**Previous optic:** Fourth-order Fresnel lens.

In 1847, Congress appropriated $4,000 for a lighthouse at Tellers Point, a narrow peninsula that juts into the center of the Hudson River from its east shore near Croton-on-Hudson. Just a year later, it was decided that Tarrytown Point, some five miles to the south, would be a more advantageous location for a light.

From the original plans

The local lighthouse superintendent, C. W. Lawrence, informed Stephen Pleasonton, the U.S. Treasury official in charge of the nation's lighthouses, that area mariners felt that nearby Kingsland Point (also known as Beekmans Point) was the best location. The property owner at Kingsland Point wanted $3,000—too much money for the two acres of land coveted by the lighthouse authorities, even though it was part of a flourishing vineyard. Congress appropriated another $7,000 for a lighthouse at Tarrytown in 1856, but the project remained stalled.

In 1881, George Brown, inspector for the Third Lighthouse District, wrote a letter to the Lighthouse Board expressing the urgent need for a light at Tarrytown. It was determined that the station could be sited offshore from Kingsland Point, and title to the property was soon obtained. Bids for construction were solicited in December 1882.

General James Chatham Duane, engineer for the Third Lighthouse

Late 1800s illustration

District, designed a caisson-type cast-iron lighthouse to be erected about a quarter-mile from Kingsland Point. The G. W. & F. Smith Iron Company of Boston created the cast-iron segments of the tower. Work began in April 1883, and by May the cylindrical cast-iron caisson was put into place and filled with concrete. The lighthouse superstructure was swiftly completed, including an interior lining of brick. The cost of the project was $20,795.

The light went into service on October 1, 1883, with a fourth-order Fresnel lens showing a fixed white light fifty-six feet above mean high water. The characteristic was later changed to fixed red and eventually to flashing red.

The diameter of the tower at its base was twenty-two feet, tapering to eighteen feet at the top. The tower was divided into four stories, each eight feet in height, topped by the watchroom and lantern. The first level contained the galley along with dining and living space, and the next three floors were the bedrooms and storage.

Inside the watchroom was automatic striking machinery for a fog bell, which was mounted on the side of the tower. The clockwork machinery was wound by the keepers in times of poor visibility, and the bell sounded a blow every twenty seconds.

To protect the lighthouse from ice on the river, 2,450 tons of rip-rap stone were piled around its base between 1889 and 1897. Although it was located a quarter-mile offshore, the lighthouse was considered a family station, and it had only twelve keepers in seventy-eight years as a staffed location. The first keeper, Jacob Ackerman, remained at the station for twenty-one years. Ackerman and his wife, Henrietta, had no children, so they kept chickens in a spare bedroom.

Ackerman was a local man who had spent more than twenty years sailing on the Hudson as the captain

## Fascinating Fact

This lighthouse is in the village of Sleepy Hollow, immortalized in Washington Irving's classic story, *The Legend of Sleepy Hollow.*

Keeper's son Larry Munzner at the lighthouse in the 1930s

of vessels plying between New York City and Albany. After serving as provost marshall in Tarrytown during the Civil War, Ackerman worked for twenty-one years as the superintendent of the Croton Aqueduct. He was fifty-seven when he became a lighthouse keeper.

Ackerman experienced a memorable storm at the lighthouse in April 1893. He wrote in the station's log: "The highest tide for many years and with a Violent Gale. The cellar of the station overflowed, and for two hours we kept carrying out water before we gained much on it." The gale swept the station's boat right off its davits and set it adrift.

Less than a week after the April storm, Ackerman heard a cry for help coming from the river. He saw that four fishermen were clinging desperately to their boat, which had capsized. Ackerman rowed to the men and quickly got them to safety, recording in the log that he received "many thanks for the . . . timely assistance in the rescue."

## SIDE TRIP:
## *Philipsburg Manor*

At Philipsburg Manor, costumed interpreters present theatrical vignettes and invite you to participate in hands-on activities of the 1700s. You can shell some beans, work flax into linen, or produce a tray of ship biscuits. Period artifacts in the 300-year-old manor house give you an understanding of eighteenth-century life. The farm includes historic breeds of oxen, cows, sheep, and chickens. The slaves' garden has vegetables and herbs for consumption, market, and medicinal purposes.

There s also a café and museum shop. Philipsburg Manor is located on Route 9 in the village of Sleepy Hollow. **For more information, see www. hudsonvalley.org or call (914) 631–8200 Monday through Friday or (914) 631–3992 on weekends.**

The Ackermans spent their fiftieth wedding anniversary in December 1898 imprisoned inside the lighthouse by ice floes. They had planned a party at the lighthouse, but the ice prevented their friends from visiting.

When he retired at the age of seventy-eight on October 1, 1904, a newspaper story reported that Ackerman's duties had "become too heavy for him." The article stated that Ackerman had been responsible for saving nineteen persons from drowning.

The writer also described the keeper's love of animals:

## SIDE TRIP: *Kykuit, the Rockefeller Estate*

Kykuit's gardens, architecture, history, and art make this a must-see. The hilltop estate was home to four generations of the Rockefeller family, beginning with John D. Rockefeller, the founder of Standard Oil. The sculpture collection in the terraced gardens includes works by Pablo Picasso, Henry Moore, Alexander Calder, and others. The galleries in the six-story stone house include Picasso tapestries.

Kykuit is reached from Philipsburg Manor, located on Route 9 in the village of Sleepy Hollow. Guided tours depart from the visitor center at Philipsburg Manor, with several tour options that allow you to tailor a visit that appeals to your interests.

**For more information, visit www. hudsonvalley.org or call (914) 631–8200 Monday through Friday or (914) 631–3992 on weekends.**

*The Captain was very fond of pets, and he had a family consisting of three cats, a dog, and two dozen chickens. The Captain has managed to keep his chickens with him winter and summer. Sometimes they fell overboard, but he managed to rescue them. In the winter time while it was terribly cold at the lighthouse he had them cared for, and he said they were good layers. One of his cats is thirteen years old, and has spent her lifetime in the lighthouse.*

Ackerman died in 1915 at the age of eighty-nine at the home of his daughter in Tarrytown. His obituary called him "one of the best-known river men on the Hudson." Of the succeeding keepers, Gus Kahlberg, formerly in charge at Eatons Neck Light Station on Long Island, served the longest stint, twenty-three years beginning in 1907.

One of the last civilian keepers was Arthur Munzner, who served from 1935 to 1939. A newspaper feature in 1939 described the life of Munzner's son, Larry, who rowed himself to a job in Manhattan every day. The lighthouse had no running water, so in the summer Larry bathed daily in the river. In winter, the family used a portable tub.

The last civilian keeper was Laureat LeClerc, a New Hampshire native who was in charge from 1943 to 1954. Years later, his daughter, Marie Leclerc Heckemeyer, recalled some happy times at the lighthouse. The parade of excursion ships passing by on the river was a pleasure, she said; at night you could sometimes hear music wafting from the vessels. She remembered a doe that swam onto the deck at the lighthouse from Kingsland Point, as well as the occasional eagle that would be seen floating by on an ice floe.

There were pleasant days, but Marie called it a "very, very lonely life." The saddest times came in October 1947 when Marie's seven-year-old brother, Andrew, drowned off the rocks near the lighthouse, only a few months after their mother had died of cancer.

Late 1800s view

The death of LeClerc's son was the second near the lighthouse in a short period of time; just a few months earlier, the four-year-old son of assistant keeper Russell Scarlett had drowned off the rocks.

A newspaper story in February 1948 reported that Coast Guard ice-breaking vessels, in the process of keeping the river clear for navigation, had piled ice up against the lighthouse and trapped the keeper inside. The ice was cleared away before the situation grew desperate.

After LeClerc left in August 1954, the station was managed by a succession of Coast Guard keepers, including Edward Brown (1954–55),

Richard S. Moreland (1955–58), and Fred Fleck (1958–59).

Moreland was profiled in a magazine article that described his life at the lighthouse with his wife, Agnes, and their two small daughters. The family enjoyed fishing right outside their home, and much of their spare time was spent watching television. It must have been a thrill for the family when Moreland had the distinction of appearing in a TV interview with Edward R. Murrow.

One of the family's most memorable nights occurred when a power failure meant Moreland had to place an emergency kerosene lamp in the tower. He had to ring the fog bell by hand for two hours that night.

The Tappan Zee Bridge, spanning the Hudson River at its widest point, was completed in 1955. The bridge, with powerful lights and a foghorn on its center span, rendered the lighthouse virtually obsolete. It was automated with reduced intensity in 1959, and two years later the light was discontinued. The last keeper, Engineman Third Class Fred Fleck, lived at the lighthouse for about five months with his wife, Claire. With the destaffing of the station, the Flecks moved to another lighthouse up the river.

Over the years, an adjoining General Motors plant expanded and filled in much of the space between the lighthouse and shore, leaving it offshore by only about fifty feet. A footbridge to the lighthouse was added in the late 1970s.

After years of abandonment, the lighthouse was acquired by Westchester County at

**Tarrytown Light in 2008**

## SIDE TRIP: *Sunnyside*

Author Washington Irving once occupied this beautiful 1835 estate. Today, costumed tour guides will tell you how Irving became America's first internationally famous author, best remembered for his story *The Legend of Sleepy Hollow* and his colorful characters, including Rip Van Winkle and Ichabod Crane. Irving arranged the garden paths, trees, and shrubs at Sunnyside, and he planted an exotic wisteria vine that's still growing.

Sunnyside is located on West Sunnyside Lane, off Route 9 in the village of Tarrytown. Hours vary at different times of the year. **For current information, visit www.hudsonvalley.org or call (914) 631–8200 Monday through Friday or (914) 591–8763 on weekends.**

the urging of community groups and historical societies. After some renovation, it was opened to the public for a celebration on October 1, 1983, exactly a century after it first went into service. Among those attending the rededication events were Marie Heckemeyer and Joseph LeClerc, the children of former keeper Laureat LeClerc.

The lighthouse may be viewed from Kingsland Point in the village of Sleepy Hollow. Follow Route 9 to Sleepy Hollow. Turn west onto Pierson Street, which becomes Bellwood Street. Turn left onto Palmer Avenue and follow to the park. A parking fee is charged at the park.

You may also view the lighthouse (along with the Little Red Lighthouse at Jeffrey's Hook) from the decks of the NY Waterways ferry from New York City to Tarrytown; call 800-53-FERRY for more information.

The lighthouse is open for occasional public tours in season, and for guided group tours by appointment; call (914) 366–5109 for the schedule and details, or write to Kingsland Point Park, Palmer Avenue, Sleepy Hollow, NY 10549. Logbooks, furnishings, and photographs inside tell the stories of family life at the lighthouse.

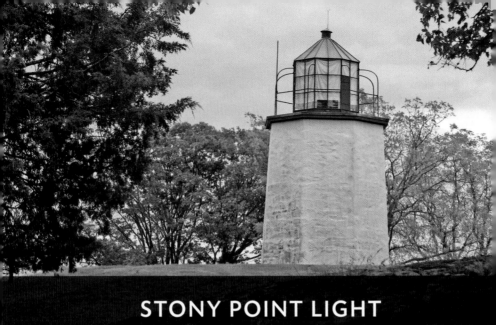

# STONY POINT LIGHT

**Accessibility:** 🚗 🚶

**Geographic coordinates:**
41° 14′ 29″ N   73° 58′ 18″ W

**Nearest town:** Stony Point. Located on the west side of the Hudson River at the Stony Point Battlefield State Historic Site.

**Established:** 1826.

**Present lighthouse built:** 1826. Deactivated: 1925. Relighted: 1995.

**Height of tower:** 30 feet.

**Height of focal plane:** 58 feet.

**Previous optic:** Fifth-order Fresnel lens (1855); Fourth-order Fresnel lens (1902).

**Present optic:** Fourth-order Fresnel lens.

**Characteristic:** White flash every 4 seconds.

Stony Point, a small peninsula on the west side of the Hudson River about twenty-five miles north of Manhattan, is best known for its historic battlefield. The Battle of Stony Point was fought on July 15–16, 1779, when Continental troops led by Brigadier General "Mad" Anthony Wayne marched south from West Point and captured a British garrison in a surprise late-night attack.

Congress appropriated $4,500 for the Hudson River's first lighthouse in 1824. Thomas Phillips was hired to build an octagonal stone lighthouse at Stony Point, along with a small stone dwelling, at a cost of $3,350. When Cornelius W. Lansing was hired as the first keeper in late October 1826, the buildings hadn't been completed. The new light went into service on December 1, 1826, not long after the opening of the Erie Canal had led to increased traffic on the Hudson.

For mariners approaching from the south, the light served to mark a narrow channel through the river to the north. Eight oil lamps, each backed by a twelve-inch reflector, produced a fixed white light. A fifth-order Fresnel lens replaced the system of multiple lamps and reflectors in 1855. It was upgraded to a fourth-order lens in 1902.

In an 1838 survey, Lieutenant George

**Fascinating Fact**

This is the oldest lighthouse on the Hudson River. Nancy Rose was the keeper here for an amazing forty-seven years (1856–1903).

W. Bache reported that the station was in poor condition. Inferior mortar had been used in the tower, and the wooden beams and rafters were decayed.

Lansing was keeper until June 1829, when he was removed for political reasons in favor of Robert

**Early 1900s view of Stony Point**

Parkerson. Lightkeeping appointments were highly political through much of the nineteenth century, and a local newspaper reported on some shenanigans in 1838. A local man reportedly was given the keeper's job in exchange for helping to get a congressman elected, in spite of his predecessor's reputation as a "worthy and attentive" attendant.

Some repairs were completed in 1841, when stone lintels and sills replaced the original wooden ones.

Inside the tower

Despite the improvements, an 1850 inspection report stated, "The lighthouse ought to be new, if nothing else." The report gave good marks to the keeper, James Miller, calling the station clean and "well-kept."

The tower has survived to the present day; a new brick dwelling replaced the original stone house in 1879. The house was rebuilt again, farther from the river, in 1938.

Alexander Rose arrived as the keeper in 1852. After he assumed his duties at the station, Rose also continued to serve as the county coroner. In 1856, Rose was helping to carry lumber for the construction of a new fog bell tower when he ruptured a blood vessel. He died just a few weeks later, and, as was often the case in the nineteenth century, his widow, Nancy, became the new keeper. Nancy Rose's great grandfather had been wounded in the Battle of Stony Point.

Along with her extensive lightkeeping duties, Nancy Rose was faced with the task of raising six children by herself. Only two of her six children,

Melinda and Alexander, reached adulthood.

An August 1895 clipping tells us of a dramatic interlude when the automatic fog bell machinery malfunctioned:

> *On one occasion, during a dense fog, she [Nancy Rose] remained for fifty-six hours at her post in the cold tower of the lighthouse, ringing the fog bell at regular intervals of half a minute. Here she remained, half frozen and without food, until the fog had disappeared.*

Only one shipwreck of note occurred near the station during the Roses' stay, when the steamer *Poughkeepsie* went aground during a March storm in 1901. Nancy Rose provided shelter and hot coffee for some forty or so passengers until they could catch a train to New York City.

For the most part, the general state of things at bucolic Stony Point was a sameness that bordered on dullness. "Nothing ever happens up here," Mrs. Rose was quoted in a 1903 article in the *New York Tribune*. "One year is exactly like another, and except for the weather, nothing changes." Her daughter, Melinda, resoundingly echoed these sentiments: "I can't remember anything that has ever happened, except once our cow died, and several times it's been bad years for the chickens."

Nancy's son Alexander, when asked if he wanted to become keeper, replied, "I'd rather pick huckleberries over the mountain for a living." Alexander Rose went on to become one of the area's leading brick manufacturers and town supervisor of Stony Point.

Nancy Rose received nothing but glowing reports from lighthouse inspectors during her tenure, and the *Tribune* called the station "exquisitely clean." But things got rather difficult for Rose toward the end of her stay, after the establishment of a state park at Stony Point. In addition to her regular duties, including the maintenance of a second light that had been added on the bell tower in 1902, the keeper was expected to provide tours of the light station for tourists.

An intruder rudely shattered the dull routine in June 1903, when Nancy Rose was 79 years old, as described in a contemporary newspaper:

> *Mrs. Nancy Rose . . . is the heroine of a combat in the historic lighthouse at Stony Point on the Hudson, in which she was pitted against a lunatic. Armed only with a poker, the woman, who . . . has attended the lighthouse half a century, bravely stood her ground and drove back her assailant. . . . He climbed into the tower, and exclaiming that the light must be torn down, started to demolish things. Mrs. Rose seized a poker and belabored him. He stood the rain of blows a moment and then fled, locking the door as he went. The old lady sounded the fog bell and secured aid.*

The stresses of age and added duties, and perhaps her scuffle with the mysterious intruder, contributed to Nancy Rose's decision to retire in 1903. She never had the chance to enjoy life away from the lighthouse, as she died the following year.

A fitting epitaph for Nancy Rose was penned in 1896 by an anonymous newspaper reporter, who wrote, "For nearly 40 years she has been found at her post of duty, with calm, quiet courage doing the task that has been set her—a lonely, thankless task, under dark or starry skies, in clear or stormy weather."

Rose's fifty-three-year-old daughter Melinda, long an unofficial assistant, took over for a while. When she resigned in 1905, Melinda Rose cited the low pay ($560 per year) and loneliness at the station in the winter. In a statement for the Stony Point Battlefield State Historic Site, Melinda later wrote, "We were at the lighthouse 53 years. In all that time there were no deaths or accidents. That speaks of faithful and conscientious service in keeping the old light burning and in ringing the warning bell in time of danger."

Frank Guyette of Vermont, a Civil War veteran, succeeded Melinda Rose as keeper in late 1905. After his wife—thirty years his junior—ran

**Stony Point Light in 2008**

away with a local policeman, Guyette raised the eyebrows of the local populace when he hired a widow named Nettie Bulson as a housekeeper.

Guyette soon found that every time he left the lighthouse, he was surrounded by inquisitive neighbors "flattening their noses against the windows." As tongues wagged, Guyette ran an ad in a local newspaper:

> *I Captain Frank Guyette of the Stony Point lighthouse, have a new housekeeper, and it seems to worry the people of Stony Point who she is.*

> *If you will please be so kind as to be in the park at 3 o'clock on Thursday, the 30th, my housekeeper and myself will take a walk through the park and you will see who she is.*

A crowd of rubberneckers showed up for the event, but the widow, apparently tired of the whole ordeal, was nowhere to be seen. Guyette vowed to hire another housekeeper, but the outcome is a mystery.

Millard Caylor was appointed keeper in 1917. A year later, a three-year-old nephew, Millard Heaphy,

SIDE TRIP:
*Van Cortlandt Manor*

This attraction, across the Hudson River from Stony Point, is a living museum illustrating the domestic life of a patriot family living in the years just after the American Revolution. The Van Cortlandts were one of New York's most prominent families. Costumed guides demonstrate blacksmithing, brickmaking, cooking, and other crafts of the period. The extensive gardens contain flowers, vegetables, and herbs that were available to American gardeners in the late 1700s. The adjacent Ferry House, built before 1750, is a rural tavern that offered food and lodging to travelers along the Albany Post Road.

Van Cortlandt Manor is located on South Riverside Avenue off Route 9 in the village of Croton-on-Hudson. **For the current hours and other information, visit www.hudsonvalley.org or call (914) 631–8200 Monday through Friday or (914) 271–8981 on weekends.**

came to live with Caylor and his wife. As he grew older, Millard Heaphy helped out with the lighthouse duties. He later recalled his uncle listening for boat horns during the night and getting out of bed to start the fog bell.

Heaphy also remembered times when the bell's mechanism would malfunction in winter, which meant that he and his uncle would take turns striking the bell with a heavy hammer every fifteen seconds. "It was a tiring job," he said.

A happier memory concerned the Fourth of July celebrations at the station. "There used to be cannons up by the light," said Heaphy. "They were from the Civil War. We'd put firecrackers in there every Fourth of July, light 'em, and run like bugger."

In 1925, while Caylor was keeper, a light on a nearby steel tower supplanted the lighthouse, but the station remained staffed. The last civilian keeper, John J. Kerr, who was born in Ireland, served from 1959 to 1968. The station was then staffed by a succession of Coast Guard keepers until 1973.

David DeLong, the Coast Guard keeper in 1969, was profiled in a local newspaper. "A lighthouse keeper's job used to be boring," he said, "but that's not the case here." DeLong, who lived at the lighthouse with his wife, Mary, and their two children, kept a twelve- to fourteen- hour watch on the maritime distress radio frequency seven days a week. The light and fog bell had already been automated by DeLong's stay; if either malfunctioned, an alarm rang in the DeLongs' home.

Terry Dixon, a twenty-two-year-old Coast Guardsman, was transferred when the station was destaffed in 1973; he had the distinction of being the last light keeper on the Hudson River.

Efforts in the 1980s and 1990s by New York state agencies led to a complete restoration of the lighthouse, culminating in a relighting in 1995. The restored lighthouse is now open to the public on days when the Stony Point Battlefield State Historic Site is in operation; the exhibits inside include a fourth-order Fresnel lens.

The museum at the Stony Point Battlefield State Historic Site showcases artifacts found on the site, including weapons used in the Battle of Stony Point. The site is open April 15 to October 2, Wednesday through Saturday from 10:00 a.m. until 5:00 p.m., Sundays from 1:00 p.m. until 5:00 p.m. It's also open on Memorial Day, Independence Day, and Labor Day, and for limited hours in the off-season.

Call (845) 786–2521 for more information, or write to the Stony Point Battlefield State Historic Site, P.O. Box 182, Stony Point, NY 10980. Website: nysparks.state.ny.us.

**Stony Point Light in the early 1900s**

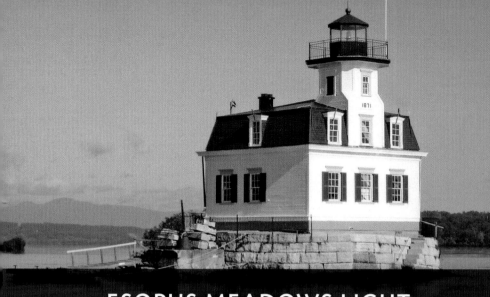

# ESOPUS MEADOWS LIGHT

**Accessibility:** 🏛 ⚓

**Geographic coordinates:**
41° 52' 06" N   73° 56' 30" W

**Nearest town:** Port Ewen. Located just west of the middle of the Hudson River, north of Esopus and south of Port Ewen.

**Established:** 1839.

**Present lighthouse built:** 1872. Deactivated: 1965. Relighted: 2003.

**Height of focal plane:** 53 feet.

**Previous optic:** Fifth-order Fresnel lens.

**Characteristic:** White flash every 4 seconds.

The mudflats known as Esopus Meadows, so named because cows supposedly grazed on pastureland there many years ago, are near the middle of the Hudson River, less than a half-mile offshore from the nearest point of land at Port Ewen. The name Esopus, by the way, is said to come from a local Indian word for a small stream or river.

To warn mariners of the shallow area, Congress appropriated a sum of $6,000 in 1837–38 for a lighthouse. Title to the site was obtained from George Terpening in August 1838 for the sum of one dollar. A relative, Jeremiah Terpening, became the first keeper.

Ried Clapp was contracted to build the lighthouse, but the project was delayed by an early frost in 1838. Work progressed the following year, and the light went into service in June 1839.

**Keeper Andrew McLintock's daughter Doris, circa 1930**

The station consisted of a bluestone dwelling with a short tower on its roof, atop a 41-by-50-foot wooden pier. An 1850 inspection report described the lighthouse as in "a dilapidated state" but clean, with the lighting apparatus in good working order.

In 1855, a sixth-order steamer lens replaced the original four lamps and corresponding fifteen-inch parabolic reflectors. Also in 1855, the Lighthouse Board reported that the southern extremity of the pier had been greatly damaged by ice coming from that direction. A triangular extension was soon added to the south side of the pier to serve as an icebreaker.

In spite of the efforts to protect it from ice, the lighthouse building was in "a ruinous condition" by the late 1860s. The Lighthouse Board's annual report of 1869 stated:

*The wooden pier upon which this lighthouse stands is in such a dilapidated state that it is feared the whole will be taken away by the ice and freshets during the coming winter. The keeper's house is unfit for occupancy in the winter, even if the foundation pier were safe enough to justify its occupancy.*

## SIDE TRIP: *Esopus Meadows Preserve*

This 93-acre park in Esopus has 3,500 feet of shoreline and is a prime spot for watching bald eagles. Two miles of wooded trails pass across varied terrain, offering views of Esopus Meadows Lighthouse and the historic Mills Mansion.

To reach the park, cross the Mid-Hudson Bridge from east to west, and take Route 9W north for 10.3 miles. Turn right on River Road and proceed 1.3 miles. The entrance is on the right. The preserve is open from dawn to dusk. Call (845) 454–7673 or visit www.scenichudson.org for more information.

On July 15, 1870, Congress appropriated $25,000 for a new lighthouse. Construction began just south of the original lighthouse during the following year, but the new structure wasn't completed until August 1872, while Jonathan Cole was the keeper. Cole was the longest serving keeper of the station, staying from 1870 to 1885.

A total of 250 forty-foot-long piles were driven into the bottom of the river, about 100 feet south of the old lighthouse. The piles were cut off three feet below mean water and then topped with a pine deck. Granite blocks were piled on top to a height of sixteen feet, and the finished round pier was forty-nine feet in diameter at the base and forty-six feet at the top.

The lighthouse, a wood-frame, seven-room dwelling with a mansard roof, was built on the pier. The building consisted of a kitchen, sitting room, an equipment room, and an indoor privy on the first floor, with three bedrooms and an equipment room for the fog bell apparatus upstairs. The light tower rises from the front end of the roof, and the lantern held a fifth-order Fresnel lens with the focal plane fifty-three feet above mean high water.

The style of the lighthouse is very similar to several others built in the northeastern United States around the same time, including Rhode Island's Pomham Rocks and Rose Island lights, and the Bridgeport Harbor Light in Connecticut. The design is credited to Albert R. Dow, a graduate engineer from the University of

Vermont. His design for the Colchester Reef Lighthouse on Lake Champlain was chosen over many entries in a national design competition run by the Lighthouse Service.

Esopus Meadows was, for many years, a family light station. Andrew McLintock, a native of Pawtucket, Rhode Island, was the keeper from 1926 to 1932. McLintock and his wife, Rebecca, welcomed a baby girl, Doris, in 1927. According to Doris (McLintock) Hubbard, Esopus Meadows was her father's first assignment after training at the Sperry Lighthouse in New Haven, Connecticut, and he always remembered the station fondly.

"In those days, the Hudson River was very different," Doris Hubbard wrote in August 2008. "The water level was much lower. In my day, fishermen hung their fishnets to dry on the low-tide mud flats. The fish, ducks, and geese helped to fill our menu. In those days, both my parents had rifles, and my nearsighted mother would always out-shoot my father. They kept the guns somewhere near the back door. When a flock of ducks flew overhead, at least one of them would land in the river, with my father rowing out to gather up our supper."

McLintock made good use of the foundation from the original 1839 lighthouse by filling it with soil and planting a vegetable garden. Around the outer perimeter he grew flowers for Rebecca.

Rebecca and Doris spent winters at their home in Rhode Island. McLintock hired an assistant to live with him in winter so that the station would never be unattended. When the river froze in winter and navigation

## "The Perfect Light"

(by Alex Ralston, nine-year-old volunteer of the Save Esopus Lighthouse Commission)

In search of the perfect light,
I have found it.
From the ruins of the old to the
tower of the new,
I have found it.
The beauty of the Maid is sleeping
and waiting
For the ones who care to find it.

came to a standstill, McLintock didn't need to light the lighthouse lamp at night. He spent much of his spare time in winter making furniture.

Once, during a trip to Staatsburg, New York, McLintock docked near a wealthy estate and saw some men replanking a large yacht. He took the leftover pieces back to the lighthouse and spent that winter making a Martha Washington–style sewing cabinet for his wife.

In the spring, when the ice would break up, it often piled up against the lighthouse foundation. "I remember the ice hitting the lighthouse like a battering ram," Doris Hubbard wrote, "with repeated booms." The whole house and foundation shook under the assault, and McLintock would remove the pendulum from a kitchen wall clock to keep the glass from breaking.

McLintock did his best to push the ice away from the wooden lighthouse, and over the years he rescued several chairs and a stool that had been left by ice fishermen to mark their favorite spots.

Two days before Christmas in 1929, McLintock noted in the log that a field of ice had struck the pier, "shaking the station considerable." McLintock had been unable to go ashore for food since December 6. In 1932, several tons of riprap stone were added around the lighthouse to improve the situation somewhat.

Animals were often a vital part of lighthouse

Manuel Resendes, right, and his wife, Ellie (Hilden)

life. According to Ruth R. Glunt's book *Lighthouses and Legends of the Hudson*, one keeper had a pet parrot that loved to chase a rolling ball across the lighthouse's tilted floor. Another keeper, John Kerr, kept a menagerie at the lighthouse that included two descented skunks and a bantam rooster. The rooster especially enjoyed riding in the boat along with a small dog when Kerr rowed to shore.

In 1937, nineteen-year-old Ellie Hilden married Manuel Resendes, the last civilian keeper at Esopus Meadows. Ellie essentially ran the station for the next seven years, as Resendes was often gone for long periods of time. Her biggest fear was thunderstorms with high winds that would sometimes extinguish the light. In winter, when the river froze, Ellie Resendes loved to skate to shore.

Under the Coast Guard, which took over the management of the nation's lighthouses in 1939, Esopus Meadows eventually became a males-only "stag station." John Olson, one of the first Coast Guard keepers

> ## Fascinating Fact
>
> The Save Esopus Lighthouse Commission has rescued this lighthouse in recent years. The leaning building was jacked up and leveled and now sits securely on new H-beams.

(1944–46), sometimes went ice sailing on the river to break up the winter monotony. Olson met his wife-to-be while assigned to Esopus Meadows.

Life on the river could be brutally harsh in winter, as one incident that was recounted in a 2003 *Lighthouse Digest* article illustrates. One member of the Coast Guard crew, Godfrey Green, was alone at the lighthouse in January 1961 when shifting ice caused the station to lose its power and telephone connection. When Green tried to use a radio to call the local Coast Guard station, it malfunctioned and caught fire.

Green eventually managed to flag down a Coast Guard vessel, and an electrician came aboard the lighthouse to repair the radio. He also managed to hook one of the electric stove's burners to a generator so that the men could enjoy a cooked meal.

There were other dangers as well. That same day, the officer in charge was ashore with his wife, who had just had a baby boy. As he walked back to the lighthouse across the ice that night, he realized he was being followed by a pack of wild dogs. After making it back safely, he requested that the crew be issued guns for protection. The request was swiftly approved.

In the station's last years, the Coast Guard keepers had six days on duty followed by three days of shore leave. A cable from shore provided electricity, but the cable was severed by ice on more than one occasion, necessitating the use of a generator.

The last crew consisted of Alfred Vaughn, Stanley Fletcher, and Lawrence Lutackas. Fletcher, who has been active in recent preservation efforts, recalls an incident when the crew rescued two young boys whose boat had caught fire. For the most part, he remembers Esopus Meadows as a quiet station compared to the offshore lights he had served on in Michigan and New York.

As the last crew prepared to leave the lighthouse in 1965, the men remembered happy summer days spent sitting in the sun, watching the boats go by. Even some of the winter memories were pleasant, such as pulling groceries back to the station on a sled. "It was a good station," said Vaughn, "but two years is enough."

The light was automated in 1965, and the navigational light was subsequently relocated to a pole nearby. The Coast Guard initially planned to demolish the lighthouse, but those plans were scrapped.

The lighthouse was abandoned after its decommissioning. Arline Fitzpatrick, niece of Ellie Hilden Resendes, started a preservation organization in 1990. Grant money was secured, and volunteers began the work of rescuing the "Maid of the Meadows." The crew of the Coast

## SIDE TRIP: *Shaupeneak Ridge Cooperative Recreation Area*

Deer, foxes, coyotes, and wild turkeys roam this 570-acre park in Esopus. Osprey and waterfowl frequent the park's Louisa Pond. There are more than 3.5 miles of trails, offering great views of the eastern Hudson River shore and the Catskill Mountains.

To reach the park, if crossing the FDR Mid-Hudson Bridge from east to west, take Route 9W north for 8.2 miles. Turn left on Old Post Road. The lower parking lot is 0.2 miles on the right. For the upper lot, follow Old Post Road to Poppletown Road, which splits off to the right. The parking area is on the left, 2.5 miles from the intersection of 9W and Old Post Road.

**For more information, call (845) 473–4440. For information on other parks and preserves on the Hudson River, visit www.scenichudson.org.**

Guard cutter *Penobscot Bay* pitched in by restoring a boom once used by the keepers to lift small boats out of the water. The crew also scraped and repainted the building along with other work.

After Fitzpatrick became ill, Pat Ralston restarted the Save Esopus Lighthouse Commission (SELC) in 1997. "I'm just so proud to be involved with this group," she once said. "All the naysayers went away, but the people that really cared and had a fire in the gut to save this lighthouse are still there."

Years of neglect, along with ice and erosion, had left the lighthouse unstable and leaning toward the east shore. Grants received from the Hudson River Improvement Fund, Greenway Heritage Conservancy, and the Department of the Interior enabled the SELC to complete structural engineering, architectural surveys and specifications, as well as emergency repairs, extensive carpentry, and the shingling of the mansard roof. The building was jacked up and leveled and now sits securely on new H-beams. The leveling of the lighthouse was partly funded by the 1996 Clean Water/Clean Air Bond Act.

After the start of the restoration process, the main goal of the SELC became ownership of the lighthouse, which had been leased from the Coast Guard on a long-term basis. The years of effort paid off on September 22, 2002, when the Esopus Meadows Lighthouse charter group (part of the

SELC) received the title for the light-house under the National Historic Lighthouse Preservation Act of 2000 pilot program.

During the transfer ceremony, Commander Keith Turo of the Coast Guard presented a symbolic key to the lighthouse to Sharon Jones, direc-tor of the SELC. Before and after the ceremony, visitors were given a tour of the lighthouse to see firsthand the work done by volunteers.

On May 31, 2003, the light was returned to the lighthouse after thirty-eight years of darkness. Stan Fletcher, one of the last Coast Guard keepers in 1965, had the honor of throwing the switch at the ceremonial relighting. More than one hundred supporters and dignitaries braved a chilly, damp night to witness the event.

Doris McLintock Hubbard, daughter of Keeper Andrew McLin-tock, visited the lighthouse in June 2004 for the first time in more than seventy years. "I walked into the old kitchen and felt at home!" she wrote. "I marveled that this old wooden

## SIDE TRIP: Staatsburgh State Historic Site

This site, within the boundaries of Mills-Norrie State Park, features a 25-room Greek Revival mansion built on the site in 1832 by Morgan Lewis and his wife, Gertrude Livingston. It was later inherited by Ruth Livingston Mills, wife of the financier and philanthropist Ogden Mills. The couple had the prop-erty enlarged in 1896 into a Beaux-Arts mansion of sixty-five rooms.

The mansion, restored to its turn-of-the-century appearance, is open for tours throughout the year. The park is located off of Route 9 in the hamlet of Staatsburg, Dutchess County.

**For more information, call (845) 889–8851 or visit nysparks.state. ny.us or www.staatsburgh.org.**

lighthouse was still standing after so many years of lonely neglect. . . . Those who labored so long and hard deserve so much credit for doing a wonderful job."

Work on the lighthouse has accelerated in recent years, and a tremendous amount has been accomplished. Some recent restoration work has been done with the help of the Ulster County Sheriff's work release program. On a brutally hot day in early summer 2006, a group of men under this program moved more than two tons of plaster to the lighthouse on a work barge and deposited the bags of plaster in designated rooms.

The interior was then plastered by Michael Armeno, an Italian-trained restoration specialist. When the plastering was completed, the walls were painted by six painters under the work release program, and a ceramic tile floor was installed in the bathroom. Two 750-gallon cisterns have been restored in the basement. New white doors to the building, replicating the originals, have also been installed.

In January 2007, the Save Esopus Lighthouse Commission became the proud owner of a forty-two-foot aluminum shallow-draft boat, the *Estuary Steward*. The boat will be used to bring public tours to the lighthouse and to assist local schools in environmental studies.

In 2008, a concrete cap was added to the lighthouse pier, and the granite blocks were repointed. With more restoration, the lighthouse will be open in the future for tours.

There are several good vantage points on shore, including the great lawn of the Mills Mansion or Norrie Point State Park in Staatsburg; the great lawn at the Wilderstein Historic Site in Rhinebeck; and the trails of the Esopus Meadows Preserve in Esopus.

For more information on the last wooden lighthouse on the Hudson River, contact the Save Esopus Lighthouse Commission, P.O. Box 1290, Port Ewen, New York 12466. Web site: www.esopusmeadowslighthouse.org.

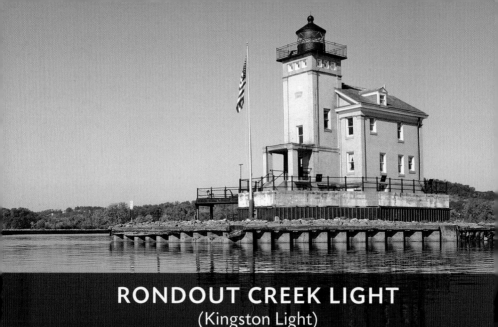

# RONDOUT CREEK LIGHT
## (Kingston Light)

**Accessibility:** ⛵

**Geographic coordinates:**
41° 55' 15" N   73° 57' 45" W

**Nearest city:** Kingston. Located at the entrance to Rondout Creek.

**Established:** 1838.

**Present lighthouse built:** 1915. Automated: 1954.

**Height of focal plane:** 52 feet.

**Previous optic:** Sixth-order Fresnel lens (1854); Fourth-order Fresnel lens (1915).

**Present optic:** 250 mm.

**Characteristic:** White flash every 6 seconds.

The Delaware and Hudson Canal, which connected the Delaware River to the Hudson River in 1828, provided a water route for the transportation of coal from mines in Pennsylvania to New York City. The canal joined with Rondout Creek between Kingston and Rosendale, New York, and then met the west side of the Hudson River.

Keeper Catherine Murdock

The confluence of the Hudson River and Rondout Creek thus became a focal point for maritime traffic. Soon, vessels of varying sizes were carrying an assortment of goods on the canal, including bricks, cement, ice, and bluestone.

To aid mariners entering the mouth of Rondout Creek, an area made treacherous by shallow tidal flats, a lighthouse was established in 1838. The original lighthouse took the form of a wood-frame dwelling topped by a lantern on a rectangular stone pier, forty-two by fifty feet in size. It was very similar to the first (1839) lighthouse at Esopus Meadows.

John McCausland succeeded the station's initial keeper, James McCausland, in December 1838. Most of the early keepers stayed for brief periods of only one to four years.

The station was inspected in 1850, when Josiah Warner was the keeper. The lantern roof was described as leaky, but the lighting apparatus was "in good order and clean." The original lighting apparatus consisted of

**Fascinating Fact**

Catherine Murdock was keeper here from 1857 to 1907. "No other place seems like home," she once said.

seven oil lamps, each backed by a parabolic reflector. The number of lamps was lowered to five in 1842, then four in 1850. A sixth-order Fresnel lens replaced the multiple-lamp arrangement in 1854.

George W. Murdock, a former employee of Sing Sing prison who was appointed keeper in 1856, moved into the lighthouse with his wife, Catherine (Parsell), and their two small children. Less than a year later, Murdock drowned during a boat trip to procure supplies. Catherine Murdock won the appointment to succeed her husband as keeper, a circumstance that was duplicated at a number of nineteenth-century light stations.

The original lighthouse was pummeled by storms and ice until it was in very poor condition by the 1860s. Pearl Rightmeyer, granddaughter of Catherine Murdock, said in a 1979 interview that her grandmother's sewing had once been interrupted when some vessels ran into the lighthouse. "One of the bowsprits came right through the wall of the dining room when my grandmother was in it," said Rightmeyer. "Luckily she wasn't killed. That was when they decided to build a stone lighthouse."

Congress appropriated $22,000 for a new lighthouse in 1866. The new two-story structure was constructed of bluestone near the location of the old one. A square granite lighthouse tower stood on the northeast side of the dwelling. The second Rondout Creek Lighthouse, known locally as the "Waterborne Castle," went into operation in 1867.

One day in 1874, two men rowed to the lighthouse in a small boat. The men told Catherine Murdock that they desired to sell their boat, and the keeper, being in need of another boat, bought it on the spot. One of her sons then rowed the men to shore.

On the next day, two detectives arrived at the lighthouse and asked the Murdocks numerous questions about their dealings with the two strange men. The men, as it turned out, were William Mosher and Joseph Douglass. The pair had acquired a widespread reputation as master thieves, and their latest scheme had been the kidnapping of a young boy, Charley Ross, in Philadelphia. The case is regarded as the first prominent kidnapping-for-ransom case in American history.

Mosher and Douglass were subsequently shot to death in an attempted robbery, and Charley Ross was never found. The Murdocks were absolved of any possible involvement in the case.

Catherine Murdock and one of her sons once helped rescue some men from the burning steamboat *Clifton*. The *Clifton*, Murdock said in an interview, presented an awesome spectacle as it passed down the river engulfed in flames.

On another occasion, Murdock

witnessed a man fall overboard from a passing vessel. Realizing that nobody on board heard the man's cries for help, Murdock swiftly grabbed a pair of oars and prepared to go to the rescue. Before she could get to the scene, her son George arrived in his small boat and pulled the man to safety at the lighthouse, where the Murdocks nursed him back to health.

In an interview, Catherine Murdock once said, "It is very pleasant at the light in summer, when we have many visitors, as many as twenty or thirty in a day. In winter, however, it is cold and dreary, and we often endure heavy and perilous storms." As a particularly bad storm was beginning in December 1878, a friend of the keeper tried to convince her to go ashore. "I'm a woman, I know," replied Murdock, "but if the lighthouse goes down tonight, I go with it."

In the predawn hours of the next morning, Catherine listened to the sounds of turbulent water and debris crashing by in the darkness. A dam up the creek at Eddyville had burst, and

### SIDE TRIP: *Hudson River Maritime Museum*

This museum, situated in the restored Rondout waterfront area in Kingston, documents the maritime history of the Hudson River, its tributaries, and the industries that developed around it. There are exhibits on the river's maritime history, a gift shop, and waterfront special events. One of the many highlights is a reproduction of Henry Hudson's aft cabin in his famous *Half Moon* exploratory vessel.

**For more information, contact the Hudson River Maritime Museum, 50 Rondout Landing, Kingston NY 12401. Web site: www.hrmm.org. Phone (845) 338–0071.**

houses and boats were swept up in the rushing waters. The lighthouse and Catherine Murdock weathered the disaster unscathed. In the aftermath, a displaced horse was seen swimming from the dike near the lighthouse to Port Ewen, more than a mile away.

In 1979, Pearl Rightmeyer recalled Catherine Murdock's work routine: "My grandmother for years would stay up to midnight to go up to the tower to keep the kerosene filled. They had nothing at night to entertain them. They had to row over to Rondout just to get the newspaper."

Catherine Murdock remained keeper until 1907, ending a remarkable fifty-year career. Very few lighthouse keepers in American history have served so long at a single station. Murdock was once asked if she was ever lonely. "Lonely? No indeed," she replied. "With all the boats going by and the view over the water, why should anyone be lonely here? But when I am away for a few days, I am always ready to come back, for no other place seems like home."

Catherine's son James was appointed as the assistant keeper in 1880, and he succeeded his mother as the principal keeper when she moved ashore in 1907. One day, during his tenure as the assistant keeper, James Murdock was credited with the rescue

Rondout Light House, Kingston, N. Y.

**Early 1900s view**

of a young man who lost control of his sailboat in high winds and heavy seas. Murdock rowed to the sailboat and boarded it, then brought it safely ashore as the seas dashed over the vessel. The boat's owner said that if it hadn't been for Murdock's quick action, he never would have reached land alive.

When James B. Murdock retired in 1923, it marked the end of a sixty-seven-year family dynasty at the lighthouse. James Murdock's 1930 obituary stated that he had saved twenty-four lives during his years at the lighthouse. Another of Catherine Murdock's sons, George W. Murdock Jr., had a long career as a marine engineer.

Two dikes were built at the entrance to Rondout Creek in the 1870s. With the addition of navigational lights on the dikes and with changes in the river channel, the lighthouse was rendered less important as a navigational aid. Shoals had extended out to the lighthouse by the early 1900s, leaving it high and dry at low tide.

In 1911, it was determined that a more substantial aid was needed

Keeper James Murdock

to mark the outer ends of the dikes on the north side of Rondout Creek. Congress appropriated $40,000 for a new lighthouse, and construction began in March 1914. The foundation consisted of a reinforced concrete pier within a steel sheet cofferdam, resting on wooden piles driven into the river bottom. A cavity at the top of the pier contained a cellar and cisterns. Atop the pier, a two-and-one-half-story yellow brick dwelling was built along with an attached forty-eight-foot-tall square brick tower.

In February 1915, during the construction project, the *Kingston Daily*

## SIDE TRIP: *Rondout–West Strand Historic District*

Rondout, the port of the town of Kingston, was once an independent town, and it still retains its independent identity. The port takes its name from Rondout Creek, a tributary of the Hudson River. The area developed quickly after the establishment of the Delaware and Hudson Canal in 1828, connecting the Delaware River to the Hudson River. Rondout was a booming town with hotels, stores, mills, and shipyards.

Much of downtown Rondout was destroyed during a phase of urban renewal in the 1960s. Around 1980, a revival of the neighborhood began with the opening of many new restaurants and shops as well as the Hudson River Maritime Museum. The attractive neighborhood offers seasonal festivals and events and has become a prime tourist attraction.

**A visitor center in the Rondout–West Strand Historic District provides exhibits and walking tour maps. For more information, visit www.kingston-ny.gov or www.hrmm.org online. For directions, visit the Hudson River Maritime Museum site at www.hrmm.org.**

*Freeman* reported that four men in the work crew narrowly escaped drowning when they attempted to cross the thin ice to Kingston. According to the newspaper story, the men fell through but were able to make it to solid ice after a desperate struggle. "None of the party suffered any serious results from their immersion," according to the account.

A fourth-order Fresnel lens in the new lighthouse produced a fixed red light from fifty-two feet above mean high water, visible for nine nautical miles. When the light went into operation on August 25, 1915, it was saluted by a vigorous horn blast from the first passing vessel, the Albany tug *Mary M.*

Work continued on the station until the following March. A 1000-pound fog bell with automatic striking machinery was also put into operation. The total amount expended under two contracts with the L. H. Bannon Plumbing and Heating and Contracting Company of Kingston was $33,575.

The lantern and deck removed from the earlier lighthouse were shipped to Rhode Island and installed on the Bristol Ferry Lighthouse. The 1867 lighthouse was offered at auction, but there were no takers. The building finally met its sad end when, after its roof fell in, it was demolished by the Coast Guard in the 1950s.

**Keeper Robert Howard with his wife and three daughters in 1944**

The station's worst tragedy occurred in 1945, when Keeper Robert L. Howard, who had been at the lighthouse for a decade, fell on the ice and suffered a head injury that led to his death.

The 1915 lighthouse remained a family station until a Coast Guard keeper was assigned in 1946. Electricity was installed in the same year. The light was automated in 1954, and the last keeper, Herman Lange, was reassigned. For some years, a civilian "lamplighter" was employed to activate the foghorn, when needed, from shore.

In 1984, the Hudson River Maritime Museum signed a twenty-year lease with the Coast Guard for maintenance of the lighthouse. After decades of neglect, much restoration was completed in the ensuing years under an agreement between the museum and the City of Kingston.

The idea for restoring the lighthouse originally came from Elise Barry, an architectural consultant in

Rhinebeck, New York. When Barry was a graduate student at the Pratt Institute in Brooklyn in 1977–78, she wrote a thesis on the adaptive reuse of the Hudson River lighthouses. State historic preservation officials invited her to be a member of the task force assembled to find ways to preserve the lighthouses.

In June 2002, under the provisions of the National Historic Lighthouse Preservation Act of 2000, ownership of the lighthouse was conveyed to the City of Kingston. The care of the property is still the responsibility of the Hudson River Maritime Museum under an agreement with the city. Much restoration of the lighthouse is planned. The building contains period furnishings and exhibits detailing the history of the light station. For the current schedule of tours, call the Hudson River Maritime Museum at (845) 338–0071 or visit www.hrmm. org online.

Fairly distant views of the lighthouse are also available from some points on shore, including Kingston Point Park. In season, you can get a good view from sightseeing cruises aboard the *Rip Van Winkle*, leaving from Kingston. See www.hudsonrivercruises.com or call (800) 843-7472.

Rondout Creek Light in 2008

# SAUGERTIES LIGHT

Esopus Creek—a tributary of the Hudson that's also known as Saugerties Creek—meets the river at the town of Saugerties, about seven miles north of Kingston and 101 miles north of New York City. Like the town of Esopus to the south, Esopus Creek was named for a local tribe of the Iroquois Confederacy.

**Accessibility:** 🚗 🚶 🛏️

**Geographic coordinates:** 42° 04' 19" N  73° 55' 47" W

**Nearest town:** Saugerties. Located at the entrance to Esopus Creek.

**Established:** 1836.

**Present lighthouse built:** 1869. Deactivated: 1954. Relighted: 1990.

**Height of focal plane:** 42 feet.

**Previous optic:** Sixth-order Fresnel lens (1854).

**Characteristic:** White light occulting every 4 seconds.

In 1627, New York's Governor Andros purchased the land that is now Saugerties from the Esopus tribe for a blanket, a piece of cloth, a shirt, a loaf of bread, and some coarse fiber. Saugerties had only twenty-one homes in 1811, but the establishment of a paper mill and an iron works on Esopus Creek in the 1820s led to increases in the population and the maritime traffic.

The creek eventually powered what has been described as the largest collection of water-powered machinery in the world. The name Saugerties is derived from a Dutch phrase meaning "sawmill on a creek."

In June 1834, Congress recognized the need for a lighthouse at the mouth of Esopus Creek, and $5,000 was appropriated for that purpose. Charles Hooster, a contractor from Saugerties, built the lighthouse at a cost of $2,988. The station was constructed at the north side of the mouth of Esopus Creek on the point of the Saugerties Flats, which extended into the Hudson River from its west bank for about a half-mile.

The original stone structure, which went into service in 1836, was built on a forty-by-forty-five-foot pier. An array of five whale oil–fueled lamps and parabolic reflectors produced a fixed white light forty-two feet above the water.

The first keeper, Abraham Persons, got into trouble in 1837 for living away from the station and hiring someone else to do the work. He was quickly dismissed, and George Keys was hired as his successor.

**Early 1900s view**

In a survey of the area's lighthouses in 1838, Lieutenant George M. Bache of the U.S. Navy was critical of the new light. "The lamps are fastened to tin pans," he wrote, "which are set upon the table; they are old and much out of repair." In 1854, the system of four lamps and fifteen-inch reflectors that had been in use was replaced by a sixth-order steamer lens.

**1886 view**

The keeper was the subject of criticism in August 1841, when Stephen Pleasonton, the U.S. Treasury official in charge of the nation's lighthouses, wrote, "The keeper should be admonished to attend better to his duty, by keeping the apparatus clean, and taking care of the public property. A second complaint will not be overlooked."

The lighthouse was destroyed by fire in November 1848 and rebuilt by 1850. An inspection report that year, when Joseph H. Bushnels was keeper, stated, "This is a new light-house, built on the old site, two stories high, with the lantern on the roof. All the lighting apparatus is second hand, but is in good working order. Reflectors are good, and everything as clean as a pin."

In the Lighthouse Board's annual report in 1855, it was noted that the timbers in the lighthouse pier were "commencing to decay." The pier had also been repeatedly injured by ice on the river, despite an ice-breaking structure at one end. The repair and strengthening of the pier was recommended at a cost of $1,136. The work was carried out by the following year. In spite of the repairs, it was necessary to rebuild the station in 1867–69, after an appropriation of $25,000.

A new round granite pier sixty feet

SIDE TRIP: *Esopus Bend Nature Preserve*

This 161-acre preserve in Saugerties offers four hiking trails at a scenic bend in the Esopus Creek and is a prime spot for birdwatching. Bald eagles, great blue herons, and egrets abound. Turkeys nest in the meadow in June. During a 2008 bird count, thirty-two species of birds were noted.

**To reach the preserve from Saugerties after crossing the Esopus Creek Bridge traveling south on Route 9W, turn right onto Overbaugh Street. Turn left onto Simmons Drive, then right onto Appletree Drive, then left onto Shady Lane. There is a small parking lot. Visit www.esopuscreekconservancy. org or call (845) 247–0664 for more information.**

station had no fog signal until a fog bell was added in 1910.

The old lighthouse was demolished in 1871, and the original pier became a public wharf. The harbor at Saugerties was improved and enlarged in 1888, and access to the lighthouse was made much easier when it was connected to the mainland by a small road atop a jetty. Extensive repairs to the lighthouse foundation pier were carried out in 1903.

Ice was a constant factor in winter life at the lighthouse; the *New York Times* reported in November 1880 that Esopus Creek was frozen from shore to shore, and boys were "skating thereon." In early January 1885, there were one hundred miles of floating ice on the Hudson between New York City and the Saugerties Lighthouse.

Kate A. Crowley became keeper in 1873, taking over the duties from her father. In 1878, a newspaper reporter described Crowley: "She is capable of any daring deed involving danger or self-sacrifice, and as to the manner in which the lighthouse

in diameter was completed in 1868, and the new combined lighthouse-dwelling was built atop the pier in 1869. The building consists of a two-story, six-room brick dwelling and an attached square brick tower. Like its predecessor, the lantern held a sixth-order lens showing a fixed white light forty-two feet above the water. The is kept, is unexcelled." Kate and her sister, Ellen, cared for their parents in addition to their lighthouse duties. "We are simply two girls trying to do our duty here in this quiet place," said Kate, "taking care as best we can of our blind father and our aged mother."

Once, during a squall, a sloop carrying bluestone capsized on the river, south of the lighthouse. Two crewmen were thrown into the turbulent water. Kate and Ellen Crowley, witnessing the accident, swiftly launched their rowboat from the lighthouse.

"The waves ran so high," according to a newspaper account, "the gale blew so madly, the thunder roared so incessantly, and the lightning flashed in such blinding sheets, that it seemed impossible for the women ever to reach the men, to keep headway, or to keep from being swamped."

Through great effort and deft rowing skill, the women reached the struggling sailors. One of the sisters grabbed hold of one of the men under his arms while the other kept the rowboat crosswise to the waves. First one man, then the other, was hauled into the rowboat. It was an act of bravery that was comparable to the feats of more famous lighthouse heroines like Ida Lewis and Kate Walker. A witness declared, "You couldn't have got any river boatmen to do what those girls did." Kate Crowley served as keeper until 1885, when her brother, James, succeeded her.

Conrad Hawk, a former U. S. Navy seaman, became the keeper in 1914 and stayed for twenty-six years. Vivian Jensen Chapin, whose father, Arthur Jensen, was keeper at Eaton's Neck Light on Long Island, wrote about visits to the Saugerties Light Station while Hawk was keeper in an article for *Lighthouse Digest* magazine.

"The light station was a comfortable home," wrote Chapin, "with airy rooms and windows letting in the soft breezes off the Hudson River. Books were everywhere, with nooks and crannies to fit into while reading. The only noise came from the boats, giving their signals coming up or down the river." According to Chapin, Hawk "enjoyed every moment of every day, making light of any mishap."

Chapin and her sister became good friends with Hawk's daughter, Ilah, who was an expert knitter. Game playing, especially card games, was another favorite activity at the lighthouse.

The keepers and their families— like lighthouse families everywhere— lived in constant anticipation of surprise visits by the local lighthouse

An early reflector and lamp are on display inside the lighthouse.

inspector, who would conduct "white glove" examinations of the premises. According to Elinor De Wire in her book *Guardians of the Lights*, the keepers at Saugerties devised a clever early warning system. A neighbor of the lighthouse had a better view of the river, and when an approaching lighthouse tender was spotted, the neighbor hung a white sheet out of an upstairs window. When the sheet was spotted, it gave the family at the lighthouse an extra half hour to tidy up.

For many years, the Lighthouse Service and then the Coast Guard maintained an attendant station at Turkey Point, about four miles from Saugerties on the west shore of the river. For twenty-eight years, the man in charge of the station was Chester Glunt, husband of Ruth R. Glunt, author and lighthouse preservationist.

In *Lighthouses and Legends of the Hudson*, Ruth Glunt described a visit with her husband to Greer Point to service the light there. As her husband completed his work, Ruth walked over a hill on the property and encountered a stout man with a large cigar. It occurred to her that he greatly resembled Winston Churchill, but it wasn't until later that she realized that she had been on Roosevelt property, and the man really was Churchill.

In her book, Ruth Glunt described the beautiful passenger steamers that passed by Saugerties Light Station. As the ships approached the lighthouse, the band would play louder, and the whistle would sound as a salute to the keeper. The keeper would wave and vigorously ring the fog bell in reply, then rush to secure his skiff before it was pounded by the heavy swells produced by the steamer.

Coast Guard personnel took over from the old civilian Lighthouse Service keepers at the Saugerties station beginning in 1940. The last Coast Guard keeper was Edward Pastorini, who arrived in 1950.

Over the decades, the shipping traffic and ferries disappeared from Esopus Creek, and the lighthouse's navigational value faded. The light

## SIDE TRIP: Seamon Park

This park, on Route 9W in Saugerties on the site of an historic mill, is home to the annual Mum Festival. The festival, inaugurated in 1965 and held the first Sunday in October, includes a variety of music, arts and crafts booths, live animals, and other attractions. Paths in the park are lined with plantings of rainbow-hued chrysanthemums, available for viewing for the remainder of the fall.

**The park, open 9:00 a.m. to dusk, features picnic tables, fireplaces, and a playground area. Call (845) 246–2321 for more information.**

was discontinued in 1954; it was replaced by a small automatic light on the opposite side of the creek. The Hudson River Conservation Society wrote many letters protesting the closing, to no avail.

Just a short time before it was destaffed, the station had been modernized with the addition of steam heat, plumbing, electricity, and telephone. According to Ruth Glunt, Pastorini had tears in his eyes the day he

## Fascinating Fact

This building, beautifully restored by the Saugerties Lighthouse Conservancy, is one of the few lighthouses where you can spend a night.

## SIDE TRIP: *Hudson Valley Garlic Festival*

The Garlic Festival, dubbed "America's Number One Food Festival" by *USA Today*, is a two-day event held at Cantine Field in Saugerties on the last full weekend in September, with music, children's activities, and arts and crafts. Also featured are the Garlic Marketplace, with tons of fresh, organically grown garlic, and the Garlic Food Court, with all manner of garlic-enhanced treats. (Garlic caramels, anyone?) **The event is sponsored by the Kiwanis Club of Saugerties, and the proceeds go back to the community in a variety of ways. For more information, visit www.hvgf.org or call the Garlic Hot Line at (845) 246–3090.**

moved his family out. A crew arrived on a lighthouse tender and proceeded to tear out the new plumbing, furnace, and fixtures. Pastorini died during the following month.

The building declined into ruin in the ensuing decades. The tower developed a tilt that left it four inches out of plumb. The second-floor roof rotted out, and the first floor was completely gone. Large gaps had opened between the granite blocks of the foundation pier. Ruth R. Glunt and architectural consultant Elise Barry succeeded in having the lighthouse listed on the National Register of Historic Places in 1978, and local interest in the structure grew.

In 1985, a new organization, the Saugerties Lighthouse Conservancy, comprised of people from both sides of the river, was formed. The organization acquired the lighthouse and the adjacent wetlands after it had reverted from the Coast Guard to the State of New York. The restoration effort soon began, and large amounts of debris were carried from the site by

A mason at work during the 1980s restoration

volunteers. Tons of sand, cement, and plaster were then transported to the site by barge. The foundation pier was repointed with hydraulic cement.

Few lighthouses have been successfully restored after falling so far into disrepair. Every face of the building required major work, and the first floor needed all new floors and partitions. More than 10,000 bricks were used to replace bricks in the tower walls that had crumbled; the mortar was formulated to match the original mortar in strength and color. The lantern was removed from the tower and completely restored. All the exterior windows, doors, and cornices were removed and rebuilt. Area craftspeople finished the building with new woodwork, plaster, and paint; plastering classes were held at the lighthouse to help defray costs. A new ventilator ball was created from the original mold and placed atop the lantern roof, replacing a ball that had been damaged. Amazingly, the restoration was completed in only four years, using public and private funds.

The heroic efforts of the Saugerties Lighthouse Conservancy climaxed with the return of a navigational light to the lighthouse on August 4, 1990, after thirty-six years in darkness. A modern acrylic optic remains in use, with a solar-powered white light occulting every four seconds.

Today, the fully restored Saugerties Lighthouse—furnished to look as it did in the early 1900s—offers public tours and special events, a small museum and gift shop, and year-round bed-and-breakfast accommodations.

Since the lighthouse reopened in 1991, there have been seven modern-day keepers. The latest is Patrick Landewe, who came to the lighthouse in 2002 after diverse experience including the supervision of conservation projects in remote locations. In the best tradition of the Lighthouse Service and the Coast Guard, Landewe records wildlife sightings, weather observations, and other news of the day in a keeper's log. You may read many of the entries online at www.saugertieslighthouse.com.

To reach the lighthouse, visitors must hike a half-mile trail through the seventeen-acre Ruth Reynolds Glunt Nature Preserve, a tidal wetlands area off Lighthouse Drive; the trail is sometimes unpassable at very high tides. Visitors are invited to visit the lighthouse grounds during the day.

Guided tours are available on summer weekends and holidays, and by appointment at other times. For more information on visiting the lighthouse or the overnight accommodations, see www.saugertieslighthouse.com or contact the Saugerties Lighthouse Conservancy, 168 Lighthouse Drive, Saugerties, NY 12477. Phone: (845) 247–0656.

Saugerties Light in 2008

# HUDSON CITY LIGHT
## (Hudson-Athens Light)

In the mid-1780s, a small village about one hundred miles north of New York City on the east bank of the Hudson River blossomed into the state's second leading port. In 1784, the port, which was previously known as Claverack Landing, was renamed Hudson after the river and its discoverer, Henry Hudson.

**Accessibility:** 🏛 ⛵

**Geographic coordinates:** 42° 15' 07" N   73° 48' 31" W

**Nearest city:** Hudson. Located near the middle of the Hudson River between Hudson and Athens.

**Established:** 1874.

**Present lighthouse built:** 1874. Automated: 1949.

**Height of focal plane:** 46 feet.

**Previous optic:** Sixth-order Fresnel lens (1874); Fifth-order Fresnel lens (1926).

**Present optic:** 300 mm.

**Characteristic:** Green flash every 2.5 seconds.

## Fascinating Fact

The city of Hudson, far from the sea, developed a prosperous whaling fleet in the 1800s.

Although Hudson was far from the sea, much of its early prominence was due to a prosperous whaling fleet. Whalers from Nantucket, fearing attack from the British, brought their ships up the river. Meanwhile, on the west side of the river opposite Hudson, the city of Athens developed into a busy shipbuilding center.

The whaling business faded by the mid-1800s, but Hudson remained an important mercantile port. Middle Ground Flats, a two-mile-long obstruction in the middle of the river between Hudson and Athens, entirely submerged during high tide, was long considered a menace to navigation. Congress finally appropriated $35,000 for a lighthouse on the flats in July 1872.

The design chosen was very similar to the Esopus Meadows Lighthouse to the south: a one-and-one-half story Second Empire–style dwelling with a tower at the front end of its mansard roof. But while the Esopus Meadows Lighthouse was constructed of wood, the Hudson City Lighthouse was built of red brick with stone lintels and quoins. A local contractor, Powley and Gage, built a granite pier for the station in 1873. The pier formed a sharp point at its north end in order to stave off ice floes.

The dwelling, built by Noone and Madden of Kingston in 1874, contained four rooms on its first floor and three bedrooms upstairs. The lighthouse tower at the front end of the dwelling held a sixth-order Fresnel lens showing a fixed white light forty-six feet above the river. The light was later upgraded to fifth-order in 1926, and the light was changed from fixed to flashing. A fog bell with automatic striking machinery was also installed. The station went into service on November 14, 1874, and the first keeper was Henry D. Best.

The lighthouse undoubtedly made travel in the vicinity safer, but accidents still occurred. In early September 1905, the small passenger steamer *Young America* collided with the ferry *George H. Power* at the southern end of the Middle Ground Flats, not far from the lighthouse. The vessels, coming from opposite sides of the river, were apparently racing for the channel in the middle of the river when they collided.

Keeper Best launched his boat, and with the assistance of the ferry crew, all the male passengers and crew from the *Young America* were rescued. Four women, however, drowned when they were pulled under by the sinking vessel.

When Henry Best died in January 1893, he was succeeded as keeper by his son, Frank. Like his father before him, Frank Best took part in a number of rescues. After he saved a boy from drowning in July 1905, Best noted in the station's log that he had received no thanks for his efforts.

Frank Best's most notable rescue occurred one day in 1912, when the passenger steamer *Isabella* collided with a tugboat near the station. The keeper rushed to the scene in his rowboat and received credit for saving eleven lives in the incident.

Frank Best died on August 10, 1918, and his widow, Nellie, assumed the lightkeeping duties until a new keeper arrived about two months later.

**Undated view of the lighthouse surrounded by ice**

During that time, Nellie's daughter rescued two men from a sinking boat near the lighthouse. William J. Murray arrived as keeper in early October 1918.

Emil Brunner was the station's last civilian keeper, serving from 1930 to 1949 at a salary of $80 per month. At first, Brunner's wife and children lived with him at the lighthouse. The Brunners' fourth child, Robert, was born at the station. For some years, the school-aged Brunner children rowed a boat or hiked across the ice to get to school.

After a few years, as the children grew older, the family moved into a house in Athens. Brunner rowed to the lighthouse nightly to perform his duties. A fifth child, Norman, was born after the move to Athens.

The *Saturday Evening Post* cover of December 28, 1946, immortalized the Brunner family in a painting by Mead Schaeffer called "Christmas at the Lighthouse." The painting depicts Brunner rowing to the lighthouse with one child and a Christmas tree on board. Anxiously awaiting the boat's arrival at the lighthouse are the keeper's wife and other children, with a few additional children added for good measure.

The light was automated in 1949; the last keeper was Coast Guardsman G. E. Speaks. For some years a "lamplighter" was paid to keep an eye on the equipment and to operate the fog bell as needed. The last lamplighter

## SIDE TRIP: *Olana State Historic Site*

Frederic Church (1826–1900), one of the Hudson River School of artists, is considered one of the most important landscape painters of the nineteenth century. He designed his Persian-style home on a hill in Hudson to take full advantage of the magnificent views of the Catskill Mountains and the river. You may tour the house and the 250 acres of the estate. The contents of the house include furniture, tapestries, rugs, paintings, sculptures, and other objects collected by Church to represent the major civilizations of the world.
**For directions and hours, visit www. olana.org or call (518) 828–0135.**

**Early 1900s view**

was William Nestlen, who performed the duties from 1966 to 1986.

In 1967, New York's Governor Nelson A. Rockefeller established the Hudson River Valley Commission, which explored possible uses of the river's lighthouses. The commission recommended the deeding or leasing of the properties to nonprofit organizations that would restore the lighthouses and work to improve public access.

The lighthouse remained essentially abandoned until the Hudson-Athens Lighthouse Preservation Society (HALPS) was formed in 1982. "If something is not done," said Craig Thorn III, chairman of the restoration committee, "the lighthouse will just crumble into the Hudson." In February 1984, the organization signed a twenty-year lease with the Coast Guard. It was the first such lighthouse lease in the Third Coast Guard District.

Ownership of the lighthouse was conveyed to HALPS in July 2000.

Restoration has focused on the years that the Brunner family spent at the lighthouse. A partial Fresnel lens is exhibited at the lighthouse, and displays in the dining room include a keeper's hat and badge, Hudson River memorabilia, and a replica of a Lighthouse Service blanket.

It was discovered in 2003 that the foundation was shifting and in need of repair. The shifts caused damage to the foundation's granite blocks, cracking the window cornices and brickwork in the lighthouse, and creating cracks in the corners of the southeastern interior walls.

Subsequent underwater examination revealed that fifty-four piles had been exposed by erosion, meaning the sediment that surrounded and supported them had been removed by the action of the water. Eight piles had

**Hudson City Light in 2008**

been sheared off completely. All the piles have also suffered decay due to fungal growths.

Funding is available for the stabilization of the timber portions of the foundation. Phase two of the project will include the replacement of sediment and riprap stone and possibly the installation of steel piling.

The Hudson-Athens Lighthouse Preservation Society holds several public open houses each season. The tours include an eight-minute ride on a pontoon boat from Athens and/or Hudson. Group and private tours may be arranged. The working fog bell is one of the last in the nation.

During many of the tours, Emily Brunner, daughter of Keeper Emily Brunner, answers visitors' questions about lighthouse life. Emily enjoys telling visitors about the time her mother made her put on a rain slicker

## SIDE TRIP: *FASNY Museum of Firefighting*

This museum depicts 300 years of firefighting history with displays of firefighting vehicles and apparatus, historic paintings, dramatic photos, badges, helmets, torches, and antique toys. Staff and retired volunteer firefighter tour guides are on hand to answer your questions. **The museum is located at 117 Harry Howard Avenue in Hudson. For more information, visit www.fasnyfiremuseum.com or call (877) 347–3687.**

and hat and sit outside during a thunderstorm; after that, Emily and her siblings never feared storms again.

For more information, visit www.hudsonathenslighthouse.org online or contact the Hudson-Athens Lighthouse Preservation Society, P. O. Box 145, Athens, NY 12015. Phone 518–828–5294.

# LOST LIGHTS OF THE HUDSON RIVER

Lighthouse, Rockland Lake, N. Y.

## Rockland Lake Light

The name of this lost lighthouse is misleading; it never stood on Rockland Lake itself. The spring-fed lake, now part of a state park, is located a short distance inland from the west bank of the Hudson River about twenty-eight miles north of New York City. The lake was the scene of a thriving ice-harvesting industry in the 1800s, and a village named Rockland Lake grew up between the lake and the river.

A shoal known as Oyster Beds, located off the Rockland Lake Landing on the river, was not an obstacle for the old-fashioned nineteenth-century sidewheel steamers and other shallow draught vessels that passed right over it. But as deeper draught vessels with propellors came into vogue, the shoal presented a danger. The Lighthouse Board stated in 1888:

> Steam vessels all lay their courses close to the Rockland Lake Landing. If there were a light and fog-signal on the shoal in question, they would, coming down stream and taking departure from Stony Point

## Fascinating Fact

This lighthouse stood with a tilt for most of its history.

Early 1900s illustration of Rockland Lake Light

> light, lay their course direct for the new light until the Kingsland Point light becomes visible, which would indicate a turning point. These courses would be reversed in going up stream. In times of snow and

West Point Light, Rockland Lake Light

*fog, a signal would obviously be invaluable.*

An examination of the site indicated that a light should be placed at the eastern end of the shoal, in about nine and a half feet of water. The board requested a Congressional appropriation of $35,000 for that purpose. The request was repeated each year until 1893, when Congress finally appropriated the needed funds.

Soundings were made at the lighthouse site in July 1893, and plans and specifications were prepared. Two concentric circles of piles, sixty-six in all, were driven into the river bottom. The outer circle, twenty-five feet in diameter, served to support the weight of the iron caisson. The inner piles were embedded in the concrete filling of the caisson cylinder.

The first two courses of the caisson were sunk into position in late May 1894, and by the end of June the caisson was ready for the addition of the lighthouse superstructure. The conical iron tower, a typical caisson sparkplug-type lighthouse of its era,

was completed in September 1894. The caisson rose seventeen feet above mean sea level, and when the lighthouse was erected, its light was thirty-seven feet above the base and fifty-four feet above mean sea level.

The lower half of the tower was painted brown, and its upper half was painted white. A fourth-order Fresnel lens was installed, showing an occulting white light that went into operation on October 1, 1894. The first keeper was Jonathan A. Miller, a Civil War veteran. A fog bell with automatic striking machinery was installed in 1896.

Between 1894 and 1897, a stone breakwater was built around the structure to serve as an icebreaker, and more than 1,000 tons of riprap stone were placed around the caisson for added protection. Despite these efforts, the tower quickly developed a pronounced tilt to the northwest. By 1897, one side was more than nine inches lower than the other.

Almost 3,000 tons of additional riprap stone was placed around the tower in the spring of 1906, but it was a losing cause. For most of the lighthouse's history, the keepers had to live life on a tilt. Ice and the shifting oyster beds on the bottom continued to plague the structure.

The *New York Times* of January 29, 1912, informs us that Robert E. Hopkins, the son of an oil tycoon, drove his automobile across the ice from Tarrytown to the Rockland Lake Lighthouse. It was the first time that feat had been accomplished. The river was so thoroughly frozen that January that it was crowded with people, cars, and horses. Thousands of skaters took advantage of the opportunity.

Finally, in 1923, the leaning tower of the Hudson was dismantled and replaced by a light on a simple skeleton tower.

## West Point Light

George Washington once called West Point "the key to the continent" because of its strategic location at an S-curve on the Hudson River. The point, on the west side of the river in the region known as the Hudson Highlands, was fortified by a garrison of Continental troops during the American Revolution. A great iron chain was extended across the river from West Point in 1778 to impede British ships. The point is best known today for the United States Military Academy located there, which was established by Thomas Jefferson in 1802.

In August 1848, Congress appropriated the modest sum of $150 for three post lights on the Hudson River: one at Catskill Reach on the west side of the river, one located two miles

## Fascinating Fact

This light stood near the United States Military Academy, established in 1802.

West Point Lighthouse, from the East Side Cliff
Hudson River, N. Y.

Early 1900s view of West
Point Light

light and fog signal traveled back and forth from their own homes. One of the keepers, A. P. Anderson, was chastised for not saluting the secretary of commerce when his steamer passed by in August 1918. The local superintendent came to Anderson's defense, explaining that the keeper lived offsite and could not be expected to be at the lighthouse at all times.

north of Hudson City at Pryme's Hook, and one at West Point. A thirty-two-foot-tall post light was established at the point in 1853, showing a fixed white light.

A proper lighthouse was built at West Point in 1872, after an appropriation of $1,500. The light was exhibited from a sixth-order Fresnel lens in the new structure beginning in September 1872. The attractive white hexagonal wooden tower was only about twenty feet tall. A fog bell with automatic striking machinery was added near the river's edge in 1888.

West Point never had a keeper's house. Local men hired to tend the

Anderson was later commended for saving two boys whose boat had capsized in 1922. Despite the fact that the station's keepers were only present a small part of the time, they were credited with several rescues over the years.

The lighthouse was demolished and replaced by a skeleton tower in 1946.

## Danskammer Point Light

Danskammer Point, a rocky point projecting into the west side of the river upstream from the Hudson Highlands, was a hazard to navigation. After a steamer ran into the point, a light and fog bell were established on June 1, 1885. The name "Danskammer" comes from a Dutch phrase meaning "devil's dancehall," so named after an early Dutch settler saw local Indians doing ceremonial dances there.

The initial lighthouse structure consisted of a wooden tower with a skeletal upper portion, with the light forty-four feet above the water. The accompanying dwelling was so tiny that most keepers chose to live in their homes nearby. The keeper from 1886 to 1919 was James H. Wiest. At first, Wiest had to row a short distance to the lighthouse, but he later was able to walk there after the area between the shore and lighthouse was filled in.

During a storm on the evening of July 11, 1914, lightning struck the metal upper portion of the lighthouse.

**Fascinating Fact**

"Danskammer" comes from a Dutch phrase meaning "devil's dancehall."

The 1925 skeletal tower at Danskammer Point

The bolt ran down the tower and entered the lower section, where it struck Wiest. The keeper was temporarily paralyzed on his right side, but he stayed at his post until daybreak.

In the morning, Wiest crawled to his house and summoned a doctor. Examination showed that the

The fog bell tower at Danskammer Point

## Four Mile Point Light

Four Mile Point is a scenic sixty-foot-high bluff located on the west bank of the Hudson, about three miles north of Athens and 120 miles above New York City. The point's name apparently comes from its distance from Hudson City. The bluff was known locally as Echo Hill because mariners used it to bounce back an echo at night or in thick fog.

lightning had passed right through him into the floor. The keeper, with the help of his wife, gradually recovered and resumed his lightkeeping duties.

In 1925, an automatic light on a black pyramidal skeleton tower with a white central column replaced the lighthouse, with the light fifty-five feet above the water.

Shallow mud flats near the river's opposite shore meant that vessels navigating the river's channel had to pass close to the point. Congress appropriated $4,000 for a lighthouse at Four Mile Point on March 2, 1829.

Early 1900s view of Four Mile Point Light

## Fascinating Fact

Some believe that Captain William Beck, an early landowner at Four Mile Point, was a pirate who buried his treasure here.

After some delay obtaining title to the site from William Jerome, a stone lighthouse tower and accompanying five-room stone dwelling were built. (According to local historian Ruth R. Glunt, the dwelling was actually built earlier by a retired sea captain and was purchased by the government.) The light went into service in 1831.

A report in November 1838 by Lieutenant George M. Bache of the U. S. Navy indicated that the lighthouse had been newly fitted with seven lamps and reflectors, arranged in two circles "so as to throw the light into the reaches up and down the river and across the channel." The system of multiple lamps and reflectors was replaced by a sixth-order Fresnel lens in 1854.

Some repairs to the buildings were completed in 1841 at the order of Stephen Pleasonton, the U.S. Treasury official in charge of the nation's lighthouses. An 1850 inspection report, when William Van Vleet was the keeper, called the station "the best kept establishment on the river."

A new tower was needed by 1880, when the original stone tower was referred to as "dilapidated and unsightly" in the Lighthouse Board's annual report. A new twenty-five-foot-tall conical cast-iron tower was erected that year with a fixed white light eighty-five feet above the river.

The lighthouse was automated with the use of acetylene gas in 1918. It was replaced by a skeleton tower near the river's edge in 1928. The old keeper's dwelling remains standing as a private home.

When the early landowner William Jerome died, he left the property near the light station to his father, who then sold it to Captain William Beck in 1839. Beck was the subject of incredible stories and legends that claimed he was a pirate who buried a fabulous treasure at Four Mile Point. Nineteenth-century spiritualists and clairvoyants attempted to locate the treasure, with no success.

There's no longer any trace of the lighthouse, but Four Mile Point is now the site of a seventy-six-acre riverfront preserve with a nature trail and a lookout providing dramatic panoramas. To visit the preserve, cross the Rip Van Winkle Bridge from east to west and turn right at the first traffic light onto Route 385 north. Continue for 7.6 miles and turn right onto Four-Mile Point Road. Follow to the parking area on the left.

## Coxsackie Light

Coxsackie Light was established in 1829 at the northeastern point of Rattlesnake Island, about two miles above Coxsackie Landing and ten miles north of Hudson City. According to historian Ruth R. Glunt, the island was probably named for the copperheads that once infested the area.

Lieutenant George Bache's report of 1838 described the station as a light on top of a keeper's dwelling, with seven lamps and reflectors. A sixth-order steamer lens was installed in 1854.

The light was useful, wrote Bache, "as a guide for vessels passing through

**Early 1900s view of Coxsackie Light**

the narrow channel formed on the one hand by the island on which the light is placed, and on the other by a flat which extends over from the eastern bank of the river."

The station was protected on its north side by a timber wall, and in the mid-1850s stone was placed on the east and west sides of the island to further protect the lighthouse from erosion. The island continued to wash away, necessitating the rebuilding of the station in 1868. The new lighthouse consisted of a two-story dwelling with a square tower at its northeast corner.

The Hoose family lived at the lighthouse for a half-century; William Hoose, keeper for thirty-two years, was succeeded by his son Frank, who stayed for eighteen years. A daughter, Emma, was born to William Hoose and his wife, Christian, in 1868.

**Fascinating Fact**

This lighthouse stood on Rattlesnake Island, named for the poisonous snakes that once lived there.

William Hoose, longtime keeper of Coxsackie Light

The lighthouse suffered an onslaught from ice on the river in early March 1902. As an ice jam broke up, huge blocks smashed through the north wall of the building and filled the first floor. The pier railing was carried away, and half the stones capping the pier were dislodged. One outhouse was carried away; the boathouse and another outhouse were crushed and moved from their foundations.

Repairs were completed that summer, and the color of the tower was changed around the same time from red to white. Ice continued to plague the station for the rest of its years, despite the addition of thousands of tons of riprap stone.

Jerome McDougall, the light's last civilian keeper, was tending a nearby light on a cluster of wooden piles one day in 1923 when the structure fell over. McDougall's heavy, waterlogged clothing made it impossible for him to swim to shore, so he held onto the bow of his skiff until a tugboat captain came to his rescue.

The lighthouse was replaced by an automatic light on a skeleton tower in 1940, and the building was soon demolished. Local people offered to buy the beautiful interior woodwork, but the government had everything burned.

## Stuyvesant Light

This station was established in 1829 on the east side of the river, at the edge of an area of mud flats about two miles north of Stuyvesant Landing. The original lighthouse was a two-story stone building, twenty by thirty-four feet, topped by a lantern. Just three years later, in March 1832, a massive ice jam broke up to the north and sent huge blocks of ice downriver, sweeping away the station.

It was one of the worst tragedies in the history of American light-houses. There were ten people inside the building at the time, including the keeper, Volkert Witbeck (sometimes spelled Whitbeck), his wife, Justine,

## Fascinating Fact

The original lighthouse here was the scene of one of the worst lighthouse tragedies in United States history, when massive ice floes crashed into the building and killed four people in March 1832.

and their three children. The keeper and his wife escaped along with one of their daughters and a visiting woman (possibly a married daughter).

Four children were lost in the disaster, including two daughters of the Witbecks, aged thirteen and fifteen. The two other children were identified as grandchildren of the keeper in a newspaper article. According to the account, the surviviors were "badly bruised."

According to one report, everyone in the lighthouse might have perished if not for the "intrepid exertions" of Charles M. Beecher, who reached the station in a small boat and rescued some of the occupants. According to local legend, there was a delay because the keeper's wife refused to leave until she finished her ironing.

After a Congressional appropriation of $5,000 in 1834, the station was rebuilt in 1835–36. A four-room stone dwelling topped by a lantern

Stuyvesant Light House, Stuyvesant, N. Y.

**Early 1900s view of Stuyvesant Light**

was constructed on a pier. In 1838, the lighting apparatus was described as five lamps with spherical reflectors, placed on two horizontal tables.

The 1836 lighthouse was surrounded on three sides by protective wooden cribwork and filled with stones. In 1855, the cribwork on the north side was described as decayed and "altogether useless," and the protective structures were improved by 1857.

In spite of the improvements, it was necessary to rebuild the station again in 1867–68. A two-story dwelling was constructed with a square lighthouse tower thirty-two feet tall at its southwest angle. A sixth-order

Fresnel lens was installed, showing a fixed white light. The old dwelling was retained as a depot for storing portable beacons that were removed from the river after the close of navigation in the winter.

Henry McAllister was the first keeper of the new lighthouse. After sixteen years, he was succeeded by his son, Edwin. Edwin McAllister and his wife, Josephine, were very active in community affairs. In her book *Lighthouses and Legends of the Hudson*, Ruth R. Glunt wrote that the McAllisters welcomed local children who loved visiting with the station's dog, pony, and parrot. If the playing children noticed the approach of a tender with a government inspector on board, they quickly headed for home.

Josephine McAllister later recalled, "My husband and I passed through many hours of trouble with high water and ice, many times the water was two feet in my room." The same ice gorge that did so much damage at the Coxsackie Light in March 1902 didn't spare this station. The westerly wall of the dwelling was smashed, and the first floor and cellar were filled with ice. In a 1938 interview, Josephine McAllister described the ordeal:

*The ice was three feet thick in the river; it rained Friday all day and night, Saturday all day and night. The fog was so thick we could not see the hill from the lighthouse. Water was coming up very fast. At two o'clock Sunday morning my husband called me up to dress as he was going to take me out. He had a rowboat in the kitchen. Water was in all the rooms. He had on high boots. We went over to the little house under the hill. Sunday morning we heard a great noise. He took the boat and a man and went to the lighthouse—what remained of it. The ice took half the lighthouse with it. He went in the rooms with a boat, where the parlor formerly was, it was gone. My piano was on the stairs, shoved there by the ice, water three feet deep in all the rooms. The old stone lighthouse, barn, hen*

*house, and bridge were gone. Water
was up to the upper floor. It took
the bedroom and reached the roof on
our side—we lost $1,000 worth of
furnishings .... They sent up eight
men to rebuild, and I had to board
them from March to November.
When I came back, I had to walk
on a ladder with two men helping
me to get into the house.*

Repairs were swiftly completed,
and in November 1902, about 500
tons of riprap stone were replaced for
added protection from ice.

In 1933, the lighthouse was
replaced by an automatic light on a
skeleton tower, and the building was
demolished three years later. Some of
the huge foundation stones were incorporated into the base of the porch of
the Stuyvesant Falls post office.

## Van Wies Point Light

Van Wies Point juts into the west side
of the river about five miles south of
Albany. The point is named for Hen-
drick Gerritse Van Wie, an early settler who built a house there in 1679.

## Fascinating Fact

William Welch kept this light for
fifty-two years, until the age of
ninety-three.

A light was established at the point
in 1854 with a twenty-one-foot-tall
stone tower at the south end of a stone
dike, showing a fixed white light. In
November of the following year, the
passenger steamboat *Francis Skiddy*
went aground on the point and the
passengers were safely removed by the
*Henrick Hudson.*

There was no keeper's house built,
so the keepers did not live on the site.
The keeper for fifty-two years (1858–
1910) was William Welch, who retired
at the age of ninety-three. Welch's
son, Franklin, succeeded his father
and remained in charge of the light
into the 1930s. The lighthouse was
later destroyed.

# Glossary

**Fresnel lens:** The 1822 invention of French physicist Augustin Jean Fresnel (pronounced "freh-NEL"). The Fresnel lens is composed of a succession of concentric rings, assembled in proper relationship, which magnify and concentrate the light and direct it in a horizontal beam.

Fresnel lenses were manufactured in as many as eleven sizes, known as orders. The order is determined by the distance of the light source to the lens. First-order Fresnel lenses (with an inside diameter of 6 feet, 1 inch) were the largest that were widely used; they were installed in many primary seacoast lights. Sixth-order lenses (with an inside diameter of 1 inch) were the smallest used in the United States., but seventh- and eighth-order lenses were used in some other countries.

Fresnel lenses were in use in all American lighthouses by the early 1860s. Some of the lenses are still in operation, but most have been removed and replaced by modern optics. Some surviving Fresnel lenses are on display in museums, such as the Maine Lighthouse Museum in Rockland, Maine.

**Height of focal plane:** The distance from the surface of the water to the center of the optic.

## Modern optics

**VRB-25:** A powerful, reliable, and compact marine rotating beacon manufactured by Vega Industries of New Zealand. The heart of the VRB-25 is a high-performance acrylic Fresnel lens.

**155 mm, 190 mm, 200 mm, 250 mm, and 300 mm optics** are essentially one-piece acrylic Fresnel lenses. They are available in clear, red, green, and yellow versions. They are usually fitted with lamp changers—devices that permit a new lamp to go into service when the existing lamp burns out.

## National Historic Lighthouse Preservation Act of 2000

**(NHLPA):** An amendment to the National Historic Preservation Act of 1966 (NHPA), this act provides a mechanism for the disposal of federally owned historic lighthouse properties. The properties are transferred to new stewards at no cost. The legislation places nonprofit entities on equal footing with federal agencies and other public bodies in the application process.

The new steward must agree to comply with conditions set forth in NHLPA and be financially able to maintain the property. The Department of the Interior is charged with choosing the most suitable applicant. In the event no new acceptable steward is found, the act authorizes the sale of the property at auction. For more on this process, see www.nps. gov/history/maritime/nhlpa/nhlpa. htm.

**Range lights:** Light pairs that indicate a specific position when they are in line. When a mariner sees the lights vertically in line, with the rear light above the front light, he is on the range line and in a safe channel.

**Sparkplug-style lighthouse:** This is a nickname for some caisson lighthouses, after their resemblance to automobile sparkplugs. Caisson lighthouses used a large cast-iron cylinder, sunk on the bottom and filled with rock and concrete to form a foundation. The superstructure is built on top of the caisson foundation. Some of these structures have also been likened to coffeepots.

# Suggested Reading

Adamson, Hans Christian. *Keepers of the Lights.* New York: Greenberg, 1955.

Bachand, Robert G. *Northeast Lights: Lighthouses and Lightships, Rhode Island to Cape May, New Jersey.* Norwalk, CT: Sea Sports Publications, 1989.

Clifford, J. Candace, and Mary Louise Clifford. *Nineteenth-Century Lights.* Alexandria, VA: Cypress Communications, 2000.

Clifford, Mary Louise, and J. Candace Clifford. *Women Who Kept the Lights.* Alexandria, VA: Cypress Communications, 2000.

Crowley, Jim. *Lighthouses of New York: Greater New York Harbor, Hudson River & Long Island.* Saugerties, NY: Hope Farm Press, 2000.

De Wire, Elinor. *Guardians of the Lights: The Men and Women of the U.S. Lighthouse Service.* Sarasota, Florida: Pineapple Press, 1995.

Floherty, John J. *Sentries of the Sea.* Philadelphia: J. B. Lippincott Company, 1942.

Gately, Bill. *Sentinels of the Shore: A Guide to the Lighthouses and Lightships of New Jersey.* Harvey Cedars, NJ: Down the Shore Publishing, 1998.

Glunt, Ruth R. *Lighthouses and Legends of the Hudson.* Monroe, NY: Library Research Associates, 1990.

Harrison, Tim, and Ray Jones. *Lost Lighthouses.* Guilford, CT: Globe Pequot Press, 1999.

Holland, Francis Ross, Jr. *America's Lighthouses: An Illustrated History.* New York: Dover Publications, 1972.

*A Light on the Hudson*. Video documentary produced by the Saugerties Lighthouse Conservancy.

Müller, Robert G. *Long Island's Lighthouses: Past and Present*. Patchogue, NY: Long Island Chapter of the U.S. Lighthouse Society, 2004.

Mylod, John. *Biography of a River: The People & Legends of the Hudson Valley*. New York: Hawthorn Books, 1969.

Noble, Dennis L. *Lighthouses & Keepers*. Annapolis: Naval Institute Press, 1997.

Rattray, Jeannette Edwards. *The Perils of the Port of New York*. New York: Dodd, Mead & Company, 1973.

Rhein, Michael J. *The Anatomy of a Lighthouse*. Barnes and Noble Books, 2000.

Snow, Edward Rowe. *Famous Lighthouses of America*. New York: Dodd, Mead & Company, 1955.

Trapani, Bob, Jr. *Lighthouses of New Jersey & Delaware: History, Mystery, Legends & Lore*. Elkton, MD: Myst and Lace Publishers, 2005.

Tuers, Rick. *Lighthouses of New York*. Atglen, PA: Schiffer Publishing, 2007.

**Magazines**

*The Keeper's Log*, published quarterly by the U.S. Lighthouse Society of San Francisco, CA. (www.uslhs.org)

*Lighthouse Digest*, published 11 times a year by FogHorn Publishing of Whiting, ME. (www.lhdigest.com)

# Lighthouse Organizations

There are many organizations that care for specific lighthouses; information on them is included in this book in the appropriate sections. There are many other local, state, and regional lighthouse preservation organizations around the United States; we urge you to support the ones near you.

The following are organizations that support the preservation of lighthouses in general:

American Lighthouse Foundation
P.O. Box 565
Rockland, ME 04841
Phone: 207-594-4174
Web site: www.lighthousefoundation.org

American Lighthouse Coordinating Committee
Web site: www.alcc.ws

New England Lighthouse Lovers
Web site: www.nell.cc

Great Lakes Lighthouse Keepers Association
P. O. Box 219
Mackinaw City, MI 49701-0219
Phone: 231-436-5580
Web site: www.gllka.com

U.S. Lighthouse Society
9005 Point No Point Road NE
Hansville, WA 98340
Phone: 415-362-7255
Web site: www.uslhs.org

World Lighthouse Society
2nd Floor, 145-157
St. John Street
London EC1V 4PY
England
Web site: www.worldlighthouses.org

# Lighthouse Index

# Photo and Illustration Credits

All the recent color photos in this book were taken by Jeremy D'Entremont, with the exceptions of the photo of Princes Bay Light on page 56, which was taken by Darlene Chisholm; the photo of Esopus Meadows Light on page 174, which was taken by John Ralston; and the photos of Hudson City Light on page 3 (top) and 203, which were taken by John Whalen. The historical images are from the collection of Jeremy D'Entremont unless otherwise indicated.

Pages 31, 43, 46, 60, 72, 80, 110, 111, 124 (top), 125, 155, 158: U.S. Coast Guard.

Pages 20, 48, 127, 130: National Archives.

Pages 54, 137, 173, 210 (bottom), 216, 218, 221: Michel Forand.

Page 56: Judy Carpenter.

Pages 86, 88: Cecile Boisvert Chenette and Celestine Boisvert O'Connor.

Pages 91, 94: Scott Schubert.
Page 132: Family of Keeper Albert Possell.

Page 133: Tom Murray and Lori Flood.

Page 146: Library of Congress, Prints and Photographs Division (3a53268).

Page 150: Library of Congress, Prints and Photographs Division (02957).

Pages 156, 158: John Ralston.

Pages 175, 178, 184, 189: Save Esopus Lighthouse Commission.

Page 191: Hudson River Maritime Museum.

Pages 194, 195, 201: Saugerties Lighthouse Conservancy.

Page 216 (top): New York Historical Society

Icons & illustratons: ©iStockphoto.com/ Tom Nulens; compass ©iStockphoto. com/www.kyc.com.uy; ©2007 Jupiter Images.

Author photo: Bob Trapani Jr.

# About the Author

Jeremy D'Entremont has been called "New England's foremost lighthouse authority." He has been research-ing, photographing, and writing about the lighthouses of New England since the mid-1980s. He launched his comprehensive web site, "New England Lighthouses: A Virtual Guide," at www.lighthouse.cc, in 1997. He is the historian for the American Lighthouse Founda-  tion, the founder of the Friends of Portsmouth Harbor Lighthouse, and vice president of the Friends of Flying Santa.

Jeremy's books include *The Lighthouses of Connecticut*, *The Lighthouses of Rhode Island*, *The Lighthouses of Massachusetts*, and *The Lighthouses of Maine*. He has edited and annotated seven new editions of books by the historian Edward Rowe Snow, including *The Lighthouses of New England*, *The Islands of Boston Harbor*, and *Storms and Shipwrecks of New England*.

He has also written more than 300 articles for publications, including *Light-house Digest* and *The Keeper's Log*, and he is the author of the "lighthouse" article in *The World Book Encyclopedia*. Jeremy's photos have been published in many magazines including *Soundings*, *Offshore*, and *Captain's Guide*.

Jeremy has lectured to groups from Connecticut to Maine, and he has nar-rated lighthouse cruises and led tour groups all along the New England coast. He lives in Portsmouth, New Hampshire, with his wife, Charlotte Raczkowski.

# About Cider Mill Press

Good ideas ripen with time. From seed to harvest, Cider Mill Press strives to bring fine reading, information, and entertainment together between the covers of its creatively crafted books. Our Cider Mill bears fruit twice a year, publishing a new crop of titles each Spring and Fall.

Visit us on the web at
www.cidermillpress.com
or write to us at
12 Port Farm Road
Kennebunkport, Maine 04046